NEW MEDIA
in the CLASSROOM

NEW MEDIA
in the CLASSROOM
Rethinking Primary Literacy

Cathy Burnett
Guy Merchant

Los Angeles | London | New Delhi
Singapore | Washington DC | Melbourne

Los Angeles | London | New Delhi
Singapore | Washington DC | Melbourne

SAGE Publications Ltd
1 Oliver's Yard
55 City Road
London EC1Y 1SP

SAGE Publications Inc.
2455 Teller Road
Thousand Oaks, California 91320

SAGE Publications India Pvt Ltd
B 1/I 1 Mohan Cooperative Industrial Area
Mathura Road
New Delhi 110 044

SAGE Publications Asia-Pacific Pte Ltd
3 Church Street
#10-04 Samsung Hub
Singapore 049483

Editor: James Clark
Editorial assistant: Diana Alves
Production editor: Victoria Nicholas
Proofreader: Jill Birch
Marketing manager: Dilhara Attygalle
Cover design: Sheila Tong
Typeset by: C&M Digitals (P) Ltd, Chennai, India
Printed in the UK

Library of Congress Control Number: 2017957930

British Library Cataloguing in Publication data

A catalogue record for this book is available from
the British Library

ISBN 978-1-5264-2084-8
ISBN 978-1-5264-2085-5 (pbk)

At SAGE we take sustainability seriously. Most of our products are printed in the UK using responsibly sourced
papers and boards. When we print overseas we ensure sustainable papers are used as measured by the PREPS
grading system. We undertake an annual audit to monitor our sustainability.

CONTENTS

LIST OF FIGURES

LIST OF TABLES

AUTHORS

Cathy Burnett is Professor of Literacy and Education at Sheffield Institute of Education, Sheffield Hallam University where she leads the Language and Literacy in Education Research Group. Her research interests focus on relationships between technology, literacy and education. A previous editor of *Literacy*, she has published widely in the areas of literacy, technology and education, including the co-edited collections *New Literacies around the Globe: Policy and Pedagogy* (2014), *Literacy, Media, Technology: Past, Present and Future* (2017) and *The Case of the iPad: Mobile Literacies in Education* (2017). She is President Elect of the United Kingdom Literacy Association.

Guy Merchant is Professor of Literacy and Education at Sheffield Institute of Education, Sheffield Hallam University. He specialises in research into digital literacy and the interrelations between children and young people, and new technologies of communication. He is widely published in international journals and is a founding editor of the *Journal of Early Childhood Literacy*. The ground-breaking *Web 2.0 for Schools* was co-authored with Julia Davies, and he has since co-edited a number of collections including *Virtual Literacies* (2013), *New Literacies around the Globe: Policy and Pedagogy* (2014), *Literacy, Media, Technology: Past, Present and Future* (2017) and *The Case of the iPad* (2017). He is active in literacy education and professional work, including writing curriculum materials and professional publications.

FOREWORD

Jackie Marsh

This is, it is frequently argued, the age of acceleration in which people feel that their worlds are speeding away beyond their control, for reasons that are not immediately apparent to them. These rapid transformations are occurring in many areas of life. Scientists, for example, report an unprecedented rate of environmental change in the anthropocene, globalisation has led to changing patterns of migration with their attendant cultural, social and economic shifts, and technological change is transforming life on a daily basis. The journalist Thomas Friedman, who has written a book about the social implications of the rapid transformations taking place in the world (Friedman, 2016), recounts that in his first reporting job in 1978, he had to queue up to use the red telephone boxes that have all but disappeared from the streets of England in order to ring through his reports for immediate publication. Today, of course, he can use email, *Skype*, texting and a range of other means to get the latest news into print – and on screens – from the remotest parts of the world. In less than four decades, communication has changed beyond all recognition.

It would be reasonable for individual teachers to feel overwhelmed by this 'runaway world' (Giddens, 1999), and to question if they are able to provide an educational experience that can prepare children for unknown futures. This book, however, provides a touchstone of good practice that is rooted in everyday classrooms, and it offers a myriad of important insights into how teachers can support children's literacy learning in these uncertain times. What is significant about this work is that it draws on rigorous, classroom-based research that has been undertaken in partnership *with* teachers and children. Thus, the participants are equal partners in the endeavour of finding meaningful and creative modes of meaning-making in the digital age.

The authors are extremely well-placed to lead us on this journey. Cathy Burnett and Guy Merchant are highly respected researchers whose work is internationally renowned in the field of new literacies studies. In this book, they draw on their research that has been undertaken over recent years, which has involved studies of the use of virtual worlds, examinations of children's use of tablets, and an analysis of the multimodal creation of films and animations, amongst other areas of interest. Fascinating vignettes from these projects are used to reflect on key principles for learning and teaching literacies in the digital age, which they draw together in their 'Charter for 21st Century Literacies'.

Initially, on encountering this work, I did question if any more frameworks for 21st century literacies were needed, given that there are various models in operation (e.g. Jenkins, Clinton, Purushotma, Robison, & Weigel, 2009). Are these various frameworks not in danger of presenting the same concepts, but in different formats, thus potentially confusing what is already a complex field of study? After reading the book, however, I recognised how wrong I was. What Burnett and Merchant's Charter offers is a sound understanding of the nature of semiotic meaning-making in a digital age, which is an element often missing in other frameworks. In other words, this Charter has a clear conception of literacy/ies as at the heart of it, rather than framing literacies as competences. In the introduction, they state that their view of literacies 'simultaneously acknowledges the centrality of lettered representation, and the importance of other semiotic systems in meaning making', and they offer a range of important insights into how communicative practices are shaped by, and in turn shape, the various technologies that are used for design, production and dissemination.

This offers a more text-based approach to a consideration of 21st century literacies than some alternative frameworks offer, which is of value to teachers who are considering how to foster children's reading, writing and communication skills in the digital age. This distinctive focus does not mean, however, that a narrow definition of text is offered. Like Kress (2003), Burnett and Merchant recognise texts as consisting of all kinds of forms that integrate a multiplicity of media and modes. They also move beyond a focus on the material to acknowledge the role that the immaterial plays in meaning-making; affect and embodied practices are key.

The structure of the book provides a strong framework for an exploration of the Charter, as each chapter illustrates one of the nine principles it contains. This enables an in-depth engagement with each principle, which is grounded in classroom examples and informed by reference to a range of theories, leading to a comprehensive account of literacies in the contemporary era. The book emphasises a need to engage in a playful approach to literacy learning, in which children can experiment and take risks in collaboration with others, using technologies in ways which lead to innovation and creativity. It is not the case, however, that there is an overly-celebratory attitude towards the role of technology in literacy lives; Burnett and Merchant acknowledge the need to engage in critical digital literacy practices in which some of the moral and ethical values at play in a 'post-truth' world are challenged and critiqued.

The book offers a strong vision of literacy learning that recognises the need to construct a 'permeable curriculum' (Dyson, 1993) in which multi-modal meaning-making connects the classroom with out-of-school domains in significant ways. The case studies outline a range of ways that this is now made possible through social media. This vision is not developed without an understanding of the material realities of teaching in a primary class-room, however, with an acknowledgement that teachers have to face a range of challenges, including faulty equipment, a lack of technical support and firewalls that block desired sites. There is no magic bullet offered to address these kinds of problems, as it is recognised that this would not only be impossible, but also undesirable if teachers are themselves to develop strat-egies that can provide a workaround to both technical and policy barriers to change. Burnett and Merchant put out a call for teachers to network with others in order to create communities of practice in which critical reflection and mutual support are key. The book, therefore, has its key audience in teachers, particularly teachers who have an intellectual curiosity about the nature of literacy in a digital age, and an ambition to create classrooms in which children can become agentive consumers and producers of a range of innovative texts and artefacts that cross digital/non-digital and online/offline domains.

There are many other audiences, however, that would do well to familiar-ise themselves with these pages. Students will find a reassuring acquaintance with, and review of, the key traditions and contemporary tropes in new lit-eracies research; researchers will be interested in the work of peers whose approach to the co-construction of knowledge with teachers is innovative and informative, and policy makers will encounter a text that will enable them to understand why there is an urgent need to move beyond an over-emphasis on alphabetic print at the expense of creating opportunities for children to become confident and confident communicators in the 21st century. Yes, this is a new epoch in which we are trying to keep up with accelerated change and immense shifts in social, cultural and economic realities, but clearly this does not mean that things are out of our control. In a seemingly runaway world, one cannot hope to succeed by clinging on to long-outdated notions of what it means to be a reader and writer, but it appears that many nation-states around the world appear to be doing just that. Yet, there are continuities as well as discontinuities in practice, and it is incumbent upon us to understand our histories and to recognise what is within our field of influence and what remains outside of it. This is, as the authors of this book point out, important not just for children's futures, but for their lives now, given they are both beings *and* becomings. Burnett and Merchant's compelling, and convincing, call to action is one that can only be ignored at our collective peril.

ACKNOWLEDGEMENTS

We are greatly indebted to our friends and colleagues, Julia Davies and Jennifer Rowsell, with whom we co-edited *New Literacies around the Globe*. That collection of research accounts described literacies in life at school and elsewhere, culminating in an initial attempt to identify some key principles of literacy in education which eventually became a *Charter for 21st Century Literacies*.

We are extremely grateful to the resourceful teachers and colleagues who we have had the pleasure to work with and have helped in refining the Charter by exploring how its principles might be applied in the classroom, particularly when policy and curriculum frameworks seem to be travelling in a rather different direction. We are also indebted to those teachers who have generously allowed us into their classrooms over many years and given us such rich insights into how digital media can help us rethink literacy in primary schools. Examples of their inspiring practices help to illuminate this book. We'd like particularly to thank Chris Bailey, Wil Baker, Jeannie Bulman, Sara Calinas, Angela Colvert, Kate Cosgrove, Adam Daley, Karen Daniels, Emma Gill, Rob Hobson, Kerry Low, Jemma Monkhouse, Richard Pountney, Dan Power, Julie Rayner, Emma Rogers, Saara Salomaa. Julia Waites, Jess Welton and all those involved with the Digital Futures in Teacher Education (DeFT) project.

We'd also like to thank Plum and The Tenth Weasley for giving us permission to include an example of the warm-hearted and constructive dialogue that typifies their exchanges on the Harry Potter Fanfiction site. Finally, we thank Jackie Marsh for generously writing the Foreword.

1

THE CHALLENGE OF
21ST CENTURY LITERACIES

This chapter will:

- provide an introduction to the book
- introduce ideas about how literacy is changing
- introduce the *Charter for 21st Century Literacies* and the nine principles that it is based upon.

At six you are already part of the world, skilfully working with the tools at hand, interacting with your environment and communicating with those who are closest to you. Your digital history trails behind you, to a time before your birth, held in pre-natal scans, health records and all the rest. As a new-born, still and moving images of you found their way onto *Instagram* and *Facebook*. Your first toys are now forgotten though once they sprang to life with flashing lights and tinny rhymes, welcoming you to the gadget world ...

New media technologies play an important role in the lives of children and young people. They are an integral part of everyday life in many parts of the world, and have been rapidly taken up in commerce, entertainment and daily communication. In education, their adoption has been rather uneven, varying between countries, regions and institutions. Although much has been written about how technology *might* or *should* change schooling, there is little principled and practical guidance for teachers – particularly for those working with children in the earlier stages of schooling. There is, however, a growing literature on how children's lives and literacy practices are influenced, inflected or transformed by digital media, and it is this body of work that we draw on in this book. Our aim in writing it is to provoke a debate about approaches to incorporating new media in schooling, to pro-vide a catalyst for change based upon what is realistic and achievable, and to argue for classroom work that reflects the changing communicative prac-tices in society at large.

Reviewing developments in policy and practice for an earlier edited volume, we concluded that there was no shortage of aspirational state-ments about how digital and online practices *might* radically change classrooms, but there was a distinct gap between these and the more conservative approaches in evidence in many curriculum documents and assessment practices around the world (Burnett, Davies, Merchant & Rowsell, 2014). Nonetheless we explored many examples of innovative teaching and learning in which teachers, sometimes working alongside researchers, were harnessing the potential of new technologies to engage children in activity that reflected the new literacies of everyday life in an authentic way. In that work we identified nine principles or orientations that underpin what, in this book, we ambitiously call a Charter for 21st Century Literacies. Using these principles, we argue, might enable colleagues to develop literacy practices in school – literacy provision that would be empowering to children and help them to have a creative and critical engagement with a range of digital media. This book explores these principles in depth and is to a large extent driven by our own expe-rience of working collaboratively with groups of primary school teachers on aspects of the Charter.

The main focus of this practical work is on situated activity – classroom activity that relates to the particular needs, interests and experiences of children in their immediate context. In this work there is often a sense of spontaneity and unpredictability, as classroom events unfold and chil-dren take the lead. Children are encouraged to be creative, improvising and collaborating in an experimental or playful manner which draws freely on their communicative resources and the materials they have access to. They work across these resources to create new meanings. This approach helps to broaden their communication repertoire and develops a creative and critical sensibility which is in step with everyday practices.

Throughout this book we adopt an expanded view of literacies which simultaneously acknowledges the centrality of lettered representation and the importance of other semiotic systems in meaning making. Engagement with new media is seen here as part of a more widespread and proliferat-ing set of communicative practices which are increasingly important to full participation in social life. This set of practices is what we mean by the *communication repertoire*. We suggest that many everyday practices involve creative, collaborative and experimental meaning making that draws on different elements of one's communication repertoire.

The Charter for 21st Century Literacies

In some respects, the principles that inform the Charter for 21st Century Literacies restate the commitments of earlier literacy scholars, and in the chapters that follow we have tried to acknowledge and reference these when appropriate. We have argued that these commitments need to be restated because of the persistence of 'old' models of literacy education (Burnett & Merchant, 2015). However, we go further than this by building on recent research in literacy, research that has drawn attention to the generative and emergent quality of the kinds of meaning making associated with digital technologies. Planning for 21st century literacies is not simply a case of substituting one set of learning goals for another. It rests on an acknowledgement that resources for communication are now richer, more diverse and more flexible than ever before. New practices, new conventions and new habits of mind are beginning to develop. We explore and exemplify this claim throughout the book.

To begin with we offer a brief summary of the nine principles of the Charter for 21st Century Literacies in order to orientate readers to our key ideas.

- **Acknowledge the changing nature of meaning making.** If we are to address the divergence between literacies in everyday life and literacy in school, we need to continually revisit our definition of the scope and range of literacy at school to reflect its changing nature.
- **Recognise and build on children's linguistic, social and cultural repertoires.** In everyday practice many children move fluidly between devices, using different modes and media, seamlessly combining both digital and non-digital interaction. This fluidity reflects their linguistic, social and cultural repertoire. For some this may involve using two or more languages, as well as the registers associated with different kinds of interaction. Recognising this repertoire and the choices it generates has implications for how we might think of an empowering literacy education. For example, it would not simply involve an incremental expansion of the kinds of texts children produce, but would also involve providing contexts in which learners could draw in open-ended ways *across* this developing repertoire: to combine and remix varied textual and linguistic practices in contexts that matter to them.
- **Acknowledge diverse modes and media.** Literacies have always been multimodal, but an explicit recognition of multiple modes can enable children to explore, develop and convey meanings in ways that might otherwise be overlooked. Opportunities to create using multiple modes help learners to explore ideas and possibilities in more nuanced ways, and digital media certainly make this easier. A specific knowledge of alphabetic representation and visual design are an integral part of this.

However, these are not separate skills but develop in tandem, and along-side other modes of communication.

- **Recognise the affective, embodied and material dimensions of meaning making.** The meanings we make are inflected by what we feel, what has just happened and who we are with, as well as how we are positioned by the people and things around us. The immediate environment, resources, personal and shared histories therefore all play a part in what children do with digital media. Literacy provision therefore needs to take account of affective, embodied and material dimensions of communicative practice.
- **Encourage improvisation and experimentation.** Although intentional design and production are important aspects of multimodal work, creative engagement is often unplanned and emergent in nature. Facilitating this sort of experimentation is based on an understanding of how meaning is made in the moment which may, or may not, result in a finished product.
- **Use playful pedagogies.** Schools have a role to play in providing risk-free environments in which children may follow passions, experiment, explore, gain feedback and consider alternatives. For teachers, this means adopting playful pedagogies and allowing work to take new or unexpected directions.
- **Create opportunities to work with the provisionality of digital media.** Although the school curriculum privileges the individual creation of fixed or final products, digital texts are often provisional, allowing them to be easily added to, reworked and remixed. Such practices have the potential to generate rich opportunities for children to reach new audiences, to give and receive feedback and to remix what others have done in ways that are both critical and creative.
- **Provide contexts that facilitate criticality.** Advocates of critical literacies argue that literacy education must address the power relationships perpetuated through and around texts through critical engagement. Calls for greater criticality have intensified in recent years and are linked to fears about internet safety, commercialism, the stereotypical depictions associated with games and virtual worlds, and the need for discerning use of online resources. Demonising the texts young people use in everyday life is likely to achieve little. Providing contexts in which young people may critically consider the practices in which they engage and how they positon themselves and are positioned by others, with opportunities to rework texts to reflect alternative experiences, is important.
- **Promote collaboration around and through texts in negotiating meaning.** Learning about new media is not just about doing things with technology, it's also about doing things with others. Recent studies provide rich insights into the ways in which children and young people

collaborate and interact on and around screens. While encouraging such collaborations, we need to be alert to the complex ways in which such interactions are managed and support children to take up such opportunities with confidence.

We believe that these principles can be used to inform classroom practice and to provide children and young people with experiences of literacy that are in step with the world that surrounds them. They also have the potential to support them in being confident and discerning users of new media. In asserting this we are not, however, claiming to have the definitive answer and will regularly refer readers to influential work that is based upon similar principles such as that of the New London Group (Cope & Kalantzis, 2000) and Jenkins et al. (2006).

A charter for a changing world?

Tsering Dolma is not at home. The house and its outbuildings are abandoned, provisions stored away for the coming winter. Although the place has an atmosphere of abandonment, there is no mystery – just a temporary absence. Water comes from a six-inch pipe running all the way up to a cistern fed by a mountain stream below Shadé, but the pipe has long since fractured. There is no water. Tsering Dolma's possessions remain, despite the locked doors. At first they're hard to make out among the red dust and mud bricks, but slowly they reveal themselves. This home is well stocked. In fact it's bristling with technology: farming implements fashioned from wands of willow, a rake, a hoe, a basket-weave cradle for flattening the earth after ploughing – all carefully stowed in the roof space or jutting out from holes in the brick work. This is the technology of subsistence farming, of a low impact bonding with the land. The only absence is Tsering Dolma herself, but she is held in a network of relationships – with locals, the monks from Phuktar, her yaks, the sheep, these basic tools and the land she scrapes her living from. What I call technology, my phone, my camera and my tablet, would be of little use to her. They would play no part. And besides, there is no electricity, no signal, no internet. And if I thought about what might improve her quality of life it would be none of this. It would be more likely to be a pair of thick woollen socks for the winter. That and someone to fix several miles of six-inch pipe. But with no utilities, public or private, that would require an attentive and caring authority – or very generous neighbours with nothing else to attend to. So perhaps now, having more or less abandoned the modernist notion of human progress, of cultural development, of economic growth and the relentless march forwards, our place in the world in all its diversity needs

(Continued)

(Continued)

to be rethought. Tsering Dolma has a different relationship with the world. Better? Worse? These evaluations hardly seem appropriate. Zanskar is a very different world and one that is separated from mine by a wide margin, and this gap throws ideas of wealth, of relationship and of technology into confusion. Care has been taken in amassing a good collection of juniper, piled on a makeshift table in a small room near Tsering Dolma's house – a different sort of plenty.

Put in straightforward terms, the idea that our communication repertoire is changing seems incontestable. But this statement comes with some caveats. First of all, it must be acknowledged that this change, although wide-reaching, is by no means universal, as the vignette above vividly illustrates. Sometimes we talk rather glibly about the global reach of technology. In fact, from a global perspective there is enormous variation in the pattern of everyday communication, as well as in access to devices, services and connectivity. Nationally, and even locally within the UK, there is considerable variation too. Apart from location, age, employment, wealth and lifestyle are among the key influences on our communication repertoire. To a greater or lesser extent, we exercise a degree of choice, but paradoxically, in many walks of life, digital communication is now essential. We know from personal experience that in a university setting it is not exactly compulsory, but it might as well be. Daily transactions between colleagues, students and support services would grind to a halt without it. In these and similar contexts, digital communication has become normalised, mobile devices commonplace – everyone has at least one – and conventions surrounding their use are gradually emerging. For instance, in some formal and informal settings there are agreements about the use of mobile devices – if someone's mobile rings in a public lecture or presentation it is usually frowned upon, yet, on the other hand, tweeting at such events has become more socially acceptable and is sometimes actively encouraged. These are issues of custom and practice, and as new communicative avenues open up, new social practices and social etiquettes are sure to follow.

The extent to which children are drawn into this changing communication environment is likely to reflect the social and material conditions of their parents or caregivers and the choices they make or the choices they are able to make. Although national surveys chart year-on-year increases in access to new media technology (see Ofcom, 2017; Pew Internet Studies, 2017) there are disparities. As an indicator of this, digital inclusion (and exclusion) has become an important area of concern (Livingstone & Helsper, 2007). But apart from this, some parents and caregivers are concerned about the possible negative effects of digital technologies and choose to regulate children's screen time. There is a literature that refers to the 'toxic' influence of new technologies on childhood (e.g. Palmer, 2006), reports on the rise of a pathological condition referred to as 'internet addiction' (Chou, Condron & Belland, 2005), some speculation on the long-term impact on eyesight and the brain (see Swain, 2011) and various commentaries on new forms of economic and cultural inequality (for example, Keen, 2015). At this point in time, however, there is little hard evidence about these negative effects. A more persuasive critique has been levelled at the domination of large global corporations, the consumerism underpinning the spread of new technologies, and the environmental degradation involved in the production and disposal of hardware (see Burnett & Merchant, 2017).

None of these critiques deny that changes are taking place, but they constitute part of an important ongoing debate about the desirability of our increased dependence on digital technology. Here, though, we are not overly concerned about whether or not this is 'a good thing'; rather we take the changes in communication repertoire as a starting point, and based upon that try to address the question of how educational provision – and particularly that aimed at the under-elevens – might adapt. It could and indeed has been argued that schools are places for face-to-face interaction, sanctuaries from a complex world and places in which the pervasive forces of new media should not be allowed to enter. We do not subscribe to this view for a number of reasons. Firstly, new media technologies are already part of children's experience: using them in schools builds on their skills and understandings of their use thereby providing important continuity with their out-of-school lives. Secondly, we believe that children should be creative and discerning users of *all* communication media and that can be best achieved by working with them in school. Thirdly, there are particular advantages, such as the ability to connect with those not present in the classroom, to share resources and to gain a direct understanding of the lives of others that is hard to achieve by other means. Using the new tools of communication enables greater participation in the social world of which they are part. Finally, new technologies already play a role in the life of the school, in their formal and informal use by teachers and school administrators and in the lives of an increasing number of children. Rather than deny this, it might be better to acknowledge it.

The question of terminology

As with any development there are challenges in finding an appropriate language to talk about the new communication practices we are concerned with in this book. So far we have used '21st century literacies', 'new media technologies', 'digital and online practices' and 'new literacies' almost interchangeably and we continue to do so throughout this book. However, there are some difficulties in this that we should not ignore. For example, we tend to think of rather different things when we think of media and literacy, but yet they are related in interesting ways (see Chapter 4 for an in-depth discussion). It is certainly the case that attempts to reflect on emerging patterns of communication have challenged what we think literacy *is*, a debate that is explored more fully in Chapter 2. Similarly, digital is not necessarily the same thing as online, and even to describe something as on-screen is ambiguous – we have only to think of the difference between touchscreens on mobiles, TV screens and ATMs to get a sense of this. Throughout the chapters in this book we attempt to navigate some of the ambiguities raised in the terms used to describe digital media, providing definitions when and where these are appropriate.

Our main emphasis is on changes to literacy provision – changes that we suggest are necessary if teaching and learning is to align with contemporary communication practices. The idea of a communication *practice* is important to us because it emphasises something that we *do* in our everyday life, whether that practice is relatively passive (as when we watch a *YouTube* clip) or more active (as in an exchange on *WhatsApp*), whether we are just looking at a *Twitter* stream or contributing by liking, tweeting or retweeting. Related to this concept of practice as action or activity, we refer throughout the book to the notion of *repertoire* which stands for all the different communication media with which we engage. Thinking about repertoire allows us to consider the differences and similarities in children's experience across different channels of communication, how they might make choices or move seamlessly between them. In this respect, we find the following definition of repertoire useful – repertoire refers to the 'conventionalized constellations of semiotic resources for taking action – that are shaped by the particular practices in which individuals engage' (Otsuji & Pennycook, 2010: 248). In other words, repertoire is firmly grounded in the individual use and practice of socially recognised communicative acts.

Locating the Charter in literacy research

This book is informed by research and scholarship in literacy studies – sometimes referred to as New Literacy Studies (Barton, Hamilton & Ivanic, 2000) – which is concerned with how meaning is negotiated between people in everyday settings rather than the cognitive skills of communication and information processing in individuals. The Charter's principles reflect three interrelated themes emerging from this field.

First, research in literacy studies sees literacy as a *social practice* (Street, 1984). It explores how literacy is used by specific groups of people in specific contexts – their interactions, the modes of communication they use and the texts they produce. We take our inspiration from work which has explored the many ways in which literacies are used for social purposes to connect people with one another. This is important because literacies allow meanings to cross spaces even when individuals do not have the power or resources to achieve this (Kell & Patrick, 2015). Research exploring children's diverse communicative practices has been particularly influential. Our first three principles therefore reflect the situatedness and diversity of literacies:

- Acknowledge the changing nature of meaning making
- Recognise and build on children's linguistic, social and cultural repertoires
- Acknowledge diverse modes and media.

Second, we are cognisant of the ways in which things such as apps, screens, devices, connectivity, arrangements of furniture and other resources play a part in how literacies get done and the kinds of meanings that get made. This *sociomaterial* perspective is helpful in articulating the complex nature of communication practices involving digital media, and this in turn has implications for how we integrate digital media in classrooms. Sociomaterialism is an umbrella term used to refer to a range of theoretical perspectives that acknowledge the web of human and non-human relations that produces the social world (Fox & Aldred, 2017). These relations affect and are affected by each other, assembling in different ways at different times. Literacy researchers have looked to sociomaterialism to describe how the social, material and semiotic combine and recombine in the moment, as meaning flows across on- and offline spaces. Our own research develops this theme. We are interested, for example, in what happens as children's screen-based activity (whether searching the internet or playing in a virtual world) intersects with what happens off-screen (e.g. spoken interactions, physical movement, proximity to other children, size and orientation of device and so on), and in how on/offscreen activity is inflected by personal histories, circumstances, moods and desires (Burnett, 2015a; Burnett & Merchant, 2016a). Our second three principles therefore acknowledge these sociomaterial relationships and the emergent nature of meaning-making:

- Recognise the affective, embodied and material dimensions of meaning making
- Encourage improvisation and experimentation
- Use playful pedagogies.

Third, a focus on *new literacies* has provided rich insights into evolving practices using digital media. Research has explored the diverse ways in which people use new media to connect with others for social, civic or political reasons, for example sharing passions, interests and concerns (Lankshear & Knobel, 2011). Studies of new media practices have highlighted the possibilities generated for activism, collaboration and creativity, but also raised concerns relating to personal vulnerability, commercial interests, discrimination and inequality. Our final three principles therefore build on particular opportunities and challenges generated through working with new media:

- Create opportunities to work with the provisionality of digital media
- Provide contexts that facilitate criticality
- Promote collaboration around and through texts in negotiating meaning.

Digital media and the primary curriculum

We hope that the discussion above has provided a convincing rationale for an increased focus on digital media in primary schools. It is important to state, however, that a focus on digital media may sit uneasily with current policy or curriculum frameworks in some locations. In England, where we are based, revisions to the national curriculum have emphasised computational thinking and computer science rather than ICT, and the curriculum for English as a subject makes no mention of digital media (DfE, 2013). Teachers' attempts to integrate digital media must jostle with pressures linked to statutory assessments for grammar, punctuation and spelling on the one hand and use of technologies for programming on the other. While an emphasis on the communicative dimensions of digital media is certainly not incompatible with these curriculum frameworks, neither is it explicitly encouraged. In other places, such as Australia, Quebec and Ontario, curriculum documentation is far more embracing of digital media (ACARA, 2013; CCEA, 2016; Ministère de l'Éducation et de l'Enseignement supérieur, 2017). Even so, pressures to address other areas of the curriculum still mean that digital media receive little attention in some classrooms. This is problematic if it means that the social, critical, creative and collaborative aspects of digital media use so central to everyday life are sidelined.

Reading this book

In the chapters that follow we take each of the nine principles in turn, using examples from everyday life and from classroom practice to develop them more fully, to expand on why they are relevant and to illustrate how they may be applied. As will already be apparent from the brief summary of the Charter at the beginning of this chapter, the nine principles are interrelated. The criticality explored in Chapter 9, for example, may well arise from the playful approaches to meaning making considered in Chapter 6. And the collaborative production of texts discussed in Chapter 10 will likely involve the review and response outlined in Chapter 8. While recognising that the nine principles interweave in practice, we present them in separate chapters as each offers a different emphasis.

The examples we use are ones we find intriguing or inspiring. Some are drawn from our own experiences while others represent the work of teachers and researchers we have worked with or whose work we have followed. Many of our examples are from schools where teachers have limited or inadequate resources and must integrate digital media alongside multiple, and often competing, expectations and demands. Most examples are from England, but we also draw from other countries to show how digital technologies have been taken up by teachers and children in different locations, and to emphasise how digital technologies are never neutral but are always placed resources (Prinsloo, 2005).

We focus on the kinds of practices that enhance opportunities for children to draw on and expand their communication repertoires in ways that are collaborative, creative and critical.

In doing so, we recognise that there are many other topics that will be relevant to teachers who are reviewing their use of digital media in classrooms. Research exploring e-books and story apps, for example, is refining our understanding of the features that are most supportive to young readers (Takacs, Swart & Bus, 2015; Rvachew, 2017), and work is being done to identify the skills and strategies associated with reading online (Leu et al., 2015). Our emphasis in this book, however, is on developing classroom media practices that usefully emulate the complex practices we see in everyday life.

As technologies inevitably evolve, new practices will continue to emerge in everyday life and we hope in schools. At the time of writing, for example, some teachers are exploring ways of using augmented and virtual reality as part of their provision, and specialist social media apps are being trialled as a way of improving home–school communication – we might well consider how such opportunities enhance or inflect children's communicative repertoires. The Charter, we suggest, has sufficient flexibility to support the development of communication repertoires drawing on a range of devices, modes and media, both those with which we are currently familiar and those yet to come.

Summary

In this chapter we have explored how literacy is changing and made the case for a focus on critical, creative and collaborative digital media practices within literacy provision. We have argued that we gain valuable insights to inform classroom provision by examining digital media practices in every-day life and have briefly outlined the Charter for 21st Century Literacies which forms the framework for the nine chapters which follow.

•••

QUESTIONS FOR REFLECTION

1. How might you begin to describe your own communication repertoire, and the role that new technology plays in this? This might include thinking about social networking sites, your use of web-based information and entertainment, and the ways in which you communicate with friends and family members.

2. How might you begin to build up a picture of the communication repertoire of children you know in a professional and domestic context? This could take the form of an informal conversation, or you might involve children in developing a list or graphic representation.

3. Reflect on a recent day spent in a primary school. How and when did you as an adult (or teacher) draw on digital technologies as part of your own communica-tion repertoire? How and when did children have access to digital technology for the purposes of communication?

•••

2

ACKNOWLEDGE THE CHANGING NATURE OF MEANING MAKING

If we are to address the divergence between literacies in everyday life and literacy in school, we need to continually revisit our definition of the scope and range of literacy at school to reflect its changing nature.

This chapter will:

- explore current tensions in the definition and description of literacy
- contrast print and screen literacies
- expand on the idea of literacy as practice.

On the Trans-Pennine train across the Peak District to Manchester the carriage is packed. There's standing room only and from here I have a good view of the other passengers. One young man must be studying for something – he's reading from a tablet while making notes on an A4 pad with green and black pens. He's got a system. The woman in the seat opposite me is reading a novel on a Kindle. It's balanced carefully on her handbag. Next to her someone is working on a spreadsheet on a chunky black laptop. The ticket collector edges his way along. Some people flash up e-tickets on smartphones, others fumble around in bags or wallets for small orange-coloured rectangles of card. The man next to me shuffles in his seat – he's reading a paperback, he's well-prepared, he uses his ticket as a bookmark. Occasionally he looks out of the window as rural Derbyshire rolls past. I tap on the screen of my phone hastily jotting down some notes. Pausing for a moment I look across the aisle. Someone's working at some music software. You can't hear what because of the Dr Dre headphones. The carriage rolls on.

This vignette takes us to an everyday setting in which we get a glimpse of contemporary literacy in the wild. Of course, it isn't a comprehensive picture – no one seems to be texting or updating their *Facebook* status for instance, but it is still recognisably 'of the moment'. And for anyone with an interest in literacy it clearly illustrates the role of both new and more established technologies in meaning making. A range of mobile devices is being used, but they take their place alongside pens, paper and books (also mobile in their own way), and sometimes in combination with one another. We can see a variety of reading and writing practices, including, of course, the reading of fiction. Fiction reading might be of interest in this context, particularly if we consider how its history is bound up with train travel, with the rise of booksellers on railway stations in the mid-nineteenth century, and even with the development of the modern paperback – itself an innovation in mobile fiction (see Lewis, 2005 for the story of Penguin paperbacks). Reading fiction, once regarded with suspicion or as a trivial or time-wasting pursuit, has now of course become a highly-valued cultural practice, often occupying pride of place in the school curriculum (Vincent, 2000). But, as our vignette illustrates, literacy can be used to describe a very broad range of practices and, as digital communication has become widespread, new kinds of literacy have emerged (Merchant, 2007a).

In what follows, we turn our attention to the changing nature of literacy, a theme that runs throughout this book, and here we provide an introduction to some of the issues that have challenged educators and scholars who seek to provide an account of these changes. To begin with it will be necessary to look directly at literacy as a concept, since it could be argued that new social and cultural conditions and the rapid influx of digital technologies have changed, or perhaps eroded, our understanding of what it means to be literate. This will lead us on to an exploration of the changing nature of literacy, and the ways in which teachers might address this in the classroom.

Defining literacy

For most readers, the idea of literacy will no doubt be closely associated with making meaning from alphabetic script, the practices that we commonly refer to as reading and writing. The development of reading and writing is one of the prime functions of schooling, and this remains true even though a considerable amount of such learning takes place outside of the school context. Indeed, for educators in most anglophone countries, literacy learning is a central concern, it is enshrined in curriculum documents and classroom activity, and is a focus for measures of pupil progress and formal assessment. Sometimes reading and writing have been referred to as the core skills of print literacy, but this can be rather misleading because they also play an important role in the post-print literacies we have been referring to. At this point, though, it is useful to adopt a slightly broader perspective and to modify our initial assumptions, to underline the fact that not all literacies are in fact dependent on an alphabetic script, and not all uses of the word literacy involve reading and writing. Partly because of all this, the term literacy can, on occasions, seem rather vague or at least hard to pin down. There are a number of reasons why this might be the case.

First, not all reading and writing is dependent on the use of an alphabetic script – why is it necessary to make this assertion? Quite simply, because some writing systems do not make use of an alphabet. Linguistic diversity is common to many people's experience, and in many parts of the UK and the rest of the world literacy involves the use of writing systems that are not based upon the letters of the alphabet. One obvious example is the use of Chinese characters, although there are plenty of other examples, too. Although it is hard to find a precise definition of what constitutes a writing system in the first place (do we, for instance, include Morse code?), for current purposes we might consider it as a symbol system used by a particular language community (or communities) to record, store and communicate meaning (see Harris, 2000). For ease of reference we call this view literacy-as-writing, because it provides a way of including some of the more commonly used writing systems that feature in the everyday lives of children and young people. As we shall see below, however, this definition does not imply that there is a direct relationship between writing and the spoken language of particular communities.

Second, it is not at all uncommon to find the word literacy applied to kinds of activity that are not directly dependent on a writing system in the first place. Examples of this include financial literacy, civic literacy and emotional literacy. Financial literacy, for instance, is described as 'experience with and knowledge about money' and its application to 'real-life situations involving financial issues and decisions' (OECD, 2017). As Barton (2007) points out, literacy in this sort of context is used metaphorically to evoke the idea of a high level of competence or fluency that may perhaps be analogous to the ways in which a literate person, by a more conventional definition, uses a writing system. Note that the definition of financial literacy given above does not make any reference to a writing or symbol system – it is one of a growing number of common uses of the term literacy. These different uses of the word have caused some confusion, particularly in educational circles, when the term *digital literacies* has been employed, with some authors using the term in this metaphorical sense to refer to a generalised sort of competence in working with computers and other devices (e.g. Eshet-Alkalai, 2004). Others, like us, use the term to refer specifically to meaning making that involves the use of new technologies (Gillen, 2014).

But even if we confine ourselves to thinking of literacy as a writing system used by a particular language community, there are all sorts of problems related not only to the difficulty in identifying and describing language communities, but also because of the varied influences that they may be subject to. For example, Punjabi speakers may become literate in a national language (Urdu or Hindi) or a non-national language (Gurmukhi), and, depending on their religious affiliation, they might also learn Arabic. In this case, which is not atypical, direct relationships between spoken and written languages are hard to find. Even, of course, where relationships are easier to map, as for instance in written and spoken English, we are effectively talking about two different, if related, language systems.

Literacy plus

The rise of screen-based communication has introduced a further complexity to how we think about literacy. Although early examples of computer-based communication were text-based (in the sense that they were dependent on written language), in a relatively short space of time, computer users were able to include both visual and audio material in websites and some messaging systems. Nowadays in popular communication channels like *Facebook* and *WhatsApp* we take these multimedia possibilities for granted. The social semiotic perspective, with its emphasis on multimodality, offers a way of describing how these different message systems interact and combine to convey meaning (see Chapter 4 for a more extended discussion). However, in emphasising how the meaning of text now often depends upon sound, image *and* writing, this perspective begins to trouble definitions of literacy (Merchant, 2007a). If reading a web-page involves synthesising meaning across different modes, then perhaps literacy is not dependent on the written word alone, but more on the 'orchestration' of modes. This is the line of argument that has been developed by Kress (2003) and others. Despite this it does not necessarily follow that the term literacy needs to extend to encompass *all* semiotic systems, but it does challenge the narrower definition of literacy-as-writing introduced above.

Taking a broader definition of literacy has meant that some scholars have included a range of semiotic systems, considering how we read images in the environment (Yamada-Rice, 2014) or how we understand moving images (Buckingham, 2003) as forms of literacy. This helps in drawing attention to how we encode and decode meaning in these different semiotic systems, suggesting the role that this may play in learning, and it certainly underscores the ways in which we privilege literacy-as-writing in our ideas about child development and formal education. Broader definitions of literacy have been influential in curriculum design, too, perhaps most notably in the multiliteracies movement (Cope & Kalantzis, 2000), but also in curriculum guidance and professional development (e.g. QCA, 2004, 2005). Surprisingly, despite these trends, some more recent curriculum reforms and accountability measures have had the effect of reigning in these developments by instantiating literacy-as-writing as a foundational and assessable skill. And in a pressurised curriculum context with demanding timetable constraints, teachers have been obliged or cajoled into adopting ever narrower practices of schooled literacy.

The high-stakes assessments that drive these practices have often become a target of professional criticism. For example, mainstream media carried the following report on a statutory test for 11-year-old children in England.

> One of the questions that caused most outcry in the spelling, punctuation and grammar (Spag) tests asked pupils to insert a pair of commas in the correct place in the following sentence: 'Jenna a very gifted singer won the talent competition that was held in the local theatre.' But many who correctly put the commas around 'a very gifted singer' failed to get a mark, to the bafflement of their teachers.

It later transpired that the children

> failed to get a mark because their commas were not curved the right way or their semi-colon was too large or not in precisely the right place ...

> (Guardian, *10 July 2017*)

Clearly a highly technical version of literacy is at work here and one that might well be seen as out of step with everyday literacy practices. For the purposes of our discussion here, however, it illustrates how literacy can cover a very broad range of preoccupations.

Changing literacies

Language change is a well-documented phenomenon, and there is a broad agreement among linguists that language varies over time and according to its context of use. Literacy, as a more codified form of language, is generally slower to change than most spoken forms of language. However, evidence suggests that we are living in a time of rapid change in literacy (see, for example, Barton & Lee, 2013). Some commentators have described this as a sort of revolution in communication, something similar in scope to the invention of the printing press. This may be a strong claim, yet one of the central concerns of this book is the expansion and diversification of literacy that has come with the spread of new technologies. Revolution or not, we can certainly note some significant changes, such as the emergence of new textual practices such as photosharing on *Flickr* and *Instagram* (Barton & Lee, 2013), videogaming (Gillen, 2014) and even the rise of more generic practices such as liking, following and the use of emojis, or the technological developments that allow us to read material such as audio books and write with voice recognition software. In this section we identify some ways of talking about these and other changes in literacy as a prelude to thinking about classroom practice. These changes are summarised in Table 2.1, and below we explain the terminology we have used.

To begin with a few words of caution are necessary. Here we are engaged in mapping some of the observable changes in literacy that are currently occurring. We are not arguing that new is necessarily *better* or that the new in some way *replaces* the old. In fact, at least at this moment in time, many of what we have labelled print literacies happily coexist with screen literacies as the vignette that opened this chapter illustrated. But this is not to deny that some things are declining in popularity or falling into disuse. We might still have a bottle of Tipp-Ex correction fluid (liquid paper) in a desk drawer, but when did we last use it? Again, the clatter of typewriters is a distant memory for an older generation – although in some parts of the world they are still used on a daily basis. Finally, there is an interesting to and fro movement between print and digital literacies – many of us still prefer to print off what we first saw on screen, and of course the text you are now reading, although composed almost entirely on screen, is available as a book, printed on paper and perhaps even stored on a bookshelf.

In Table 2.1 we start by contrasting the changes in the *material form* of the texts we read and write. In short what we are referring to is the basic stuff that you need – the starter pack as it were. This perspective invites us to consider some interesting economic issues. Entry level costs are much higher for the newer literacies, but after that initial investment, different economies come into play. Certainly, we may have the additional cost of word-processing or e-book software, but then e-books themselves are cheaper than print versions. Then again, setting up an email account is fairly straightforward, and once we have done that communication is free (apart from the hidden and relatively small cost of connectivity); so-called snail-mail, on the other hand, carries a cost for each transmission. Considering material form also introduces another interesting shift. In older literacies different text types were often distinguished by differences in materiality. The glossy magazine, the academic tome and the birthday card are each distinct in look and feel. The move to screens has ushered in increased convergence in the sense that each of these text types, perhaps with the exception of the birthday card, can be viewed on one device. Related to this then are differences in how and where the text itself appears. We refer to these as *display characteristics*. Here we might reflect that with ink and paper texts we always need to have the original or a copy of the text at hand, whereas with a digital device we can call it up almost at will – assuming of course that we have stored it on our device or 'in the cloud'.

When we refer to *inscription tools* we are concerned with the physical and technological work that has to be done in order to produce text in the first place. It has often been said that the history of literacy is intimately tied to its technology of production (Merchant, 2017) and this is certainly the case with the emergence of digital tools. In the history of literacy, the development of paper is as significant as the development of the printing press, whereas the invention of the keyboard has carried over from early telegraph machines, through typewriters to computer keyboards and their touchscreen counterparts. There are some fundamental differences here though as we move from pen and paper to keyboard and screen. In the former we use our embodied knowledge of handwriting to make an impression on the surface of the page. Working on screen requires a different sort of dexterity in which we select letters and in the case of predictive text whole words which are instantaneously translated to pixels and displayed to look like 'print' text. Here we use the technical word *tokens* to refer to those individual elements of text, since this enables us to capture something more than the letters of the writing system, be that whole words, icons (such as emojis) or larger chunks of text (as in cutting and pasting).

In some contexts, *commenting* on text plays an important role, too. This could include replying to a handwritten note, reviewing and giving feedback or, in educational contexts, marking. Traditionally this has involved annotations or marginalia, whereas now, most word processing packages include review functions (in-text comments or tracked changes). Of course a more fundamental shift towards online commenting has developed in some digital formats. Examples of this are the reader or user comments that are found beneath *YouTube* videos, online news features or on consumer sites. These can work to recontextualise or problematise the initial piece, they may turn into a sort of discussion or even go off in new and unexpected directions. Vasquez's (2014) study of online consumer reviews is a scholarly examination of this phenomenon and one which contains a wealth of entertaining examples.

These developments in commenting raise interesting issues about the fixity or completeness of a text. If comments are considered as part of the text, then it is not exactly complete until a final comment has been added. And, of course, if the original text can be revised at will, as it can, for example, in a blog post or webpage, then what is seen at any point in time is only one iteration of the text. This is very different from more traditional conceptions of written text, which despite some changes with respect to draft versions or revised editions, is seen to be relatively fixed. An extreme version of this can be seen at work in *Twitter*. Not only is the text continually aggregating like an ongoing multiparty conversation, but also participants have a unique or personalised view, dependent on who or which hashtag they follow (see Gillen & Merchant, 2013).

The textual fluidity that characterises *Twitter* has interesting implications for saving, archiving and *storage*. It operates according to a different logic. Comparisons with paper records or the various ways of storing or cataloguing books are hard to make. Digital texts are saved by us (assuming we remember to do so) on our hard drive or on an external server. Forgetting to save, once the curse of many writers' lives, is now less of a problem with the introduction of autosaving routines of the sort we encounter in *GoogleDocs*.

Finally, we consider two features of composition or design that we have already mentioned earlier. The first of these relates to the wider topic of multimodality (see Chapter 4). In Table 2.1, we use the term *semiotic combination* to refer to the ways in which we can include other modes alongside written communication. As we noted earlier, although multimodality is not a new phenomenon (Kress, 2003), the ease with which this can now be done has characterised the emergence of new kinds of textual composition. Last of all, we draw attention to the ways in which we can reference within and between texts. Traditionally, footnotes, endnotes and bibliographic referencing have been the stock in trade, and although these are still adhered to in some formats – this book would be a case in point – hyperlinked text performs a similar and sometimes more sophisticated function in digital and online text.

Table 2.1   Mapping changes in literacy

	Print	Screen
Material form	Book, magazine, paper	Desktop, laptop, mobile device
Display characteristics	Ink on paper	Pixels on screen
Inscription tools	Pencils, pens, typewriters	Keyboard, touchscreen, mouse, touchpad
Tokens used	Formed by hand or by mechanical operation	Selected from keyboard or menu
Changing the text	Erasers, liquid paper, scissors and glue	Copy, paste, delete
Commenting	Marginalia	Review functions, public comments
Storage	Books, folder, files	Saved, or autosaved
Semiotic combination	Sketches, photographs	Audio, still and moving image
Cross-referencing	Footnotes, bibliographies	Hyperlinks

These aspects of literacy are one way of trying to map the changes that are associated with new media, but for us they can only ever be a partial account, and this is because they portray literacy as a particular kind of thing, in terms of its textual and material form, disconnected from the uses to which it is put in the contexts of social interaction. After all, as we argued in Chapter 1, literacy is a social practice and the changes which we have described only exist when they are taken up in human communication.

Changing practices

The concept of social practice is a helpful way of thinking about the roles that technology and literacy play in our everyday lives and in the lives of the children we work with. It helps in understanding *how* literacies are used for social purposes, to connect people with one another for example or to record and store information, and *what* processes and technologies are involved. The word practice also evokes the notion of context(s), or *where* these processes are occurring, and *who* they involve. For the theorist Schatzki (2002), practices are 'organized nexuses of activity', that involve bodily 'doings', 'sayings' and 'relatings'. These doings, sayings and relatings take place in the human interactions that constitute social life (Schatzki, 2002: 56). Practices also include 'things and their use' (Reckwitz, 2002: 5) – the material arrangements of this social activity. As we saw in the last chapter, this notion of practice has become central to our understanding of the social and sociomaterial characteristics of literacy. From this point of view, changes in literacy associated with its textual and material appearance are only part of the story. Such changes influence and are influenced by the wider social, political and economic contexts they are embedded in, resulting in changing practices.

As an example of this, we turn our attention to literacy-related toys for toddlers and pre-school children. In a study of how small-scale electronic and digital technology takes shape in the lives of babies and toddlers we looked at the ways in which new technologies have become enmeshed with early play and exploration – activities that are infused with ideologies about early learning and the development of literacy (Merchant, 2015a). For example, we looked at the VTech First Steps Babywalker, which is an 'electronic learning product' (vTech, 2017) retailing in shops and supermarkets around the world. The babywalker incorporates digital components into its pedagogical design. When the toddler (or adult) presses the 'a' key it lights up and a voice says: 'a is for apple' and this is followed by the sound of biting an apple. In other words, the babywalker produces a new kind of practice, building on familiar toys like push-and-pull brick trolleys, by introducing a digital element – even though the version of literacy incorporated might seem rather anachronistic.

A more explicitly educational activity is promoted by the *Endless Alphabet* app. This tablet app develops letter matching and early spelling skills using simple touch movements to drag and drop letters to name everyday objects. When an onscreen letter is touched, it increases in size and is animated, dancing around and adopting an animal-like form. Moving the letter (by moving the finger) activates the phonic sound that it usually makes. Putting a letter in the correct place elicits cheers and applause. And when all the letters are in place, there's a short animation followed by a spoken definition. Figure 2.1 shows the screen for the word 'dye'. Completing the correct spelling of this word ends with: 'When you dye something you are changing its colour. Usually you dye hair or fabric.' The Endless Alphabet delivers a very familiar set of literacy teaching activities – letter recognition, letter matching and spelling using phonics, the screen background even represents slightly crumpled lined paper. It also involves what has been described as the effortless performance of human touch (Robles-de-la-Torre, 2006: 24). But there is, behind all this, a level of sophistication in the design, a training in operating touchscreens and the possibility of learning literacy without the direct involvement of a co-present adult. In short there are some practices here, which include the manipulation and use of a tablet, that are relatively-speaking new and certainly qualitatively different from something like an alphabet board game.

Figure 2.1   Screen for the word 'dye'

Source: © Originator Inc.

In this study it was noted that despite the ubiquitous presence of digital communication in the everyday lives of many young children, the toys and games that they are likely to encounter are designed to deliver a skills-based view of literacy – learning that focuses on vocabulary, letter recognition and spelling. These are marketed to parents as a way of providing a 'good start' for their children, and often involve touchscreen technology and digitally mediated sound effects and voices. Yet, as a result of this, from the outset, babies and toddlers are involved in different kinds of digital practices, play episodes begin to look rather different and toys take on new functions.

Of course, this sort of play is only one possible kind of experience in the broad range of practices that a young child might be involved in. Most children will have considerable experience of different media when they begin school, whether this is driven by their own interest or through that of their siblings and caregivers, and the totality of these experiences constitutes their communication repertoire, as we saw in the previous chapter. These repertoires will vary considerably and children may engage in different kinds of practices associated with different domains of their lives. In a study of children's uses of mobile phones in Cape Town, South Africa, Kell (2017) noted how phones were used very differently in an after-school reading club to how they were used by children in their social lives outside school. Recognising and building on this repertoire is an important first principle if we are going to develop creativity and criticality. Along with this, practitioners may also want to encourage children to reflect on the role played by technology in their own lives and how this may be changing what they can do.

Summary

In this chapter we have acknowledged the many ways in which 'literacy' is understood, ranging from different takes on the nature of reading and writing to loose applications of 'literacy' to refer to skills or competences across a range of subjects and activities. We have clarified the use of 'literacies' in this book to refer to meaning making that involves the use of new technologies. We have described some of the possibilities made available through digitisation and pointed to various ways in which literacies have changed in recent years and are continuing to change. We end by emphasising that changing literacies are not just the result of evolving technologies; they are produced through practices as people take up digital technologies in different ways in particular settings.

QUESTIONS FOR REFLECTION

1. Reflect on the communicative resources you have drawn on at different times of your life: as a child, as a teenager, now. Consider these in relation to Table 2.1. How have these different communicative practices drawn on material form, display characteristics, inscription tools and so on?

2. How has your own communication repertoire shifted? And/or expanded? And/or contracted? For what kinds of reasons has this happened, e.g. linked to available technologies, to different practices or to different events or phases in your life?

3

RECOGNISE AND BUILD ON CHILDREN'S LINGUISTIC, SOCIAL AND CULTURAL REPERTOIRES

In everyday practice many children move fluidly between devices, using different modes and media, seamlessly combining both digital and non-digital interaction. This fluidity reflects their linguistic, social and cultural repertoires. For some this may involve using two or more languages, as well as the registers associated with different kinds of interaction. Recognising this repertoire and the choices it generates has implications for how we might think of an empowering literacy education. For example, it would not simply involve an incremental expansion of the kinds of texts children produce, but would also involve providing contexts in which learners could draw in open-ended ways *across* this developing repertoire: to combine and remix varied textual and linguistic practices in contexts that matter to them.

This chapter will:

- address children's differing levels of experience with digital media
- consider the ways in which schools can learn about and build on this experience
- explore how teachers can support children in engaging productively, creatively and safely with new technology.

Kenny crawls behind Hannah, his teacher, moving away to kneel at a nearby book trolley. As Iona and Hannah continue with the iPad story he struggles to hold a board book, it slips from his grip and turns upside down. He tries

(Continued)

(Continued)

to open it and then it slides through his hands and drops to the floor. Hannah and Iona continue to look at the iPad, listening to the story. With careful support from Hannah, Iona gradually builds the confidence to turn pages on the app herself. Only some of her efforts meet with success. In Figure 3.1 we can see Iona practising her page-turning while Kenny looks somewhat dejected. Meanwhile, though, he maintains contact with Hannah by applying firm pressure with his right shoe, as if to ensure that she doesn't forget he's still there. Perhaps as a result, Hannah looks across at Kenny to re-engage his attention. It seems to work, and Iona shifts to the right as Kenny approaches from the other side. Although Hannah tries to keep the narrative going with Iona there is now competition for her attention. As Kenny kneels down, he extends his forefinger as if to tap the screen. Hannah angles the iPad in his direction. Kenny moves his hand at the last minute so that when it makes contact with the iPad the thumb comes to rest on the home button, which he then presses decisively. The story comes to an abrupt end and Kenny looks up at the camera grinning mischievously.

Figure 3.1   Looking at the iPad

This is a commentary on some video observation in an early years' setting from the summer of 2014 when story apps on tablets were just beginning to attract the attention of practitioners and researchers. It offers some intriguing insights into young children's literate behaviour and their engagements with tablet technology. We can see, for example, how the app provides a context for something that looks rather like a familiar story-sharing routine. There are particular bodily movements and gestures involved, and there is something about holding, something about pointing and something about tapping and swiping that is highly relevant to discussions about this sort of technology – these are given a more detailed treatment elsewhere (e.g. Merchant, 2015b; Burnett et al., 2017). In this observation we see two toddlers and their teacher engaging with an iPad, each in a rather different way. We use this short sequence to draw attention to some important issues in the take-up of new technology in educational contexts.

Iona, who in the screenshot (Figure 3.1) is sitting on her teacher's lap, appears to be quite happily enjoying the Peppa Pig story. She also seems quite at ease with the tablet, and has her forefinger extended in what could be described as an 'appropriate' fashion. This all suggests that she is favourably disposed to this sort of story experience, and that she is becoming familiar with using a tablet in this way. However, we know nothing about her prior experience of touchscreen technology, or for that matter whether sitting with her teacher and joining in – whatever the activity – was what was actually important to her in that moment. Similarly, if we turn our attention to Kenny, who crawls around in the background most of the time, we can only guess at his underlying motivations and whether that decisive final contribution of turning the app off was intentional or not. His handling (or mishandling) of the board book raises similar issues, of course. The fact that he doesn't demonstrate early print literacy skills – in this case holding a book and turning its pages – may not necessarily mean that these skills are absent from his repertoire. They just weren't apparent on that occasion. So, it is only with more prolonged engagement and observation of children's digital literacies that we can really get a sense of what they can do with technology and through that build on their understanding. In other words there has to be a limit to claims about what today's children can do with new technology.

The ubiquity of new literacies has led many commentators to make generalisations about children's experience of meaning making with new media, many of which lack any substantial evidence. Large-scale surveys of things like smartphone ownership and internet access (such as those produced by Ofcom and Pew Internet Studies), and of more specific digital practices such as videogaming and virtual world play (e.g. KZero, 2015) are often used to support such generalisations. Although these data provide helpful indications of trends and make a significant contribution to our understanding of the wider sociocultural environment, they inevitably tend to gloss over diversity and difference in children's digital lives and their everyday experiences of digital literacy.

Digital capital

Many influential studies of literacy have drawn attention to the different ways in which the literacies of the home are either valued and recognised or undervalued and overlooked in the school context. Often drawing on social theory and ideas of social and cultural capital (Bourdieu, 1992), these studies argue that the literacies of low-status social groups receive less recognition in formal educational contexts than those of dominant groups. For example, Heath's linguistic ethnography provides a powerful illustration of how the practices and language resources of some children are recognised as a valuable resource, creating advantage for these children at the expense of others whose experiences of language and literacy may be overlooked (Heath, 1982). Although this patterning of inequality may not be the result of the *intentional* actions of teachers or schools, the effects of privileging things like book ownership and mainstream media, combined with a curriculum in which a particular set of literate behaviours is made visible, may work to the disadvantage of some children.

As we showed in Chapter 1, the recent diversification of literacy practices adds complexity to the picture. Merchant (2007b) suggests that it might be helpful to start thinking in terms of 'digital capital' – the resources or assets that some children have, or could acquire, to prepare them for the future. The difficulty with this position is that, for reasons beyond their control, schools may find it challenging to identify children's digital resources in the first place. In her study of Monument Valley, Maine (2017) shows how children drew in different ways from their cultural knowledge in making sense of this game, which was unfamiliar to most of them, and how as a result they navigated the text in different ways. For one pair play was strategic, drawing on their experience of playing other similar games to solve the problems presented; another pair was caught up in the story and characters, while others did whatever they needed to do to finish the game. Maine explores how children bring diverse understandings with them to gameplay and how these, in turn, help to frame their play. In the context of this study these diverse understandings were unproblematic, but a persistent failure to recognise aspects of children's communication repertoire can create or sustain inequality.

Since experiences of new media are intimately tied in with the social practices of families and communities these are important considerations for disadvantaged or marginalised groups. Razfar and Gutiérrez suggest that children now inhabit semiotic worlds that are:

> Dramatically different than the predominantly print-based one in which their parents became literate. The new literacy environment is broader, more dynamic, more fluid, multi-layered and multimodal.
>
> *(Razfar & Gutiérrez, 2013: 65)*

The work of Gutiérrez and her colleagues has been influential in highlighting how this impacts on children from minority groups, drawing attention to the hybrid, multimodal practices of dual-language learners. For example, in her study of children of Mexican descent living in the US, she observes how their language is

> textured with Spanish, English, and African-American dialect, as well as hip-hop vernacular; and multimodal signs ranging from familiar cultural artifacts to popular culture and school-related icons adorn their notebooks, backpacks, and drawings.
>
> *(Gutiérrez et al., 2011: 235)*

In other words the communication repertoire of these children is complex and diverse, patterned by a whole range of influences. Anglo-normative educational provision that focuses on mainstream culture works to silence these rich communicative resources, and can end up making children appear deficient.

What children know

Over a decade ago, a small-scale study of 10–11-year-old children's internet uses suggested, perhaps unsurprisingly, that children were using the internet in diverse ways and for very different purposes and that these were linked to their own particular interests and their family circumstances (Burnett & Wilkinson, 2005). More recently we have observed similar variation in young children's iPad use. This underscores the need for more fine-grained analyses, such as those generated by the TAP project (Marsh et al., 2015). The TAP project included, among other things, data on tablet ownership, competence and daily usage as well as more in-depth case studies. However, with the range of devices that is currently available, the rapid diffusion of new software and the variable and changing nature of parental control, there will always be an element of instability in this sort of data. Perhaps the key point rests on an acknowledgement of the wide spread of digital literacies and the recognition that they make up a significant part of everyday communicative practice. Children are likely then to have different levels of interest, experience and access to such practices.

At first sight it might seem rather tricky to build curricula on such an uneven ground of experience, but in fact it is no different to any other form of learning. In this respect, there are obvious parallels with early print literacy. For example, studies of the home reading environment and book ownership have provided us with useful contextual information (Levy, 2010), but it is only through collaborative professional work with parents and careful observational assessments of children that teachers are able to design learning that extends experience. The same applies to what we are referring to as 21st century literacies. Building in *Minecraft* might be an almost obsessive preoccupation for one child while parody videos may be an interest for another, but some may prefer drawing, book reading or making dens in the garden. Primary school teachers are already skilled at recognising differences in interest and experience and building on them. The change in orientation which we are arguing for in this book is to extend this teaching approach to encompass the kinds of literacies that are currently important in the lives of children and in the wider social context, to invest in a wider textual repertoire

Extending children's textual repertoire

Designing activities that allow children to work together using a range of different media provides teachers with opportunities to observe different preferences and levels of experience and to intervene sensitively to promote learning. The collaborative working this entails enables children to share skills and to learn from each other. This approach emphasises the close and reciprocal relationship between assessment and learning, and underlines the significance of ongoing informal assessment. In contrast, some commentators have argued in favour of more formal assessments of new literacies (Hammett, 2007; Burke & Hammet, 2009; Leu et al., 2013), based partly on the fact that high-profile and wide-scale assessment are important in steering practice. For as long as assessments that favour print-based literacy dominate education – or so the argument runs – the take-up of new literacies in the classroom will be limited. Although we have some sympathy with the argument, it has its limitations. Firstly, it assumes a power-coercive model of curriculum development, one that is driven by assessment (see Moss, 2017, for a commentary on the problematic nature of this model). This runs counter to the ideas of professional integrity and empowerment that we subscribe to. But secondly, it implies a relatively stable set of skills that are amenable to measurement. Given the rapidly changing nature of these literacies, as outlined in Chapter 1, stability is the very thing that eludes us. But also, if new literacies are highly contextualised, socially constructed and involve the complex layering of semiotic modes, they are always likely to be beyond the reach of assessment as we currently know it.

For those teachers accustomed to using prescriptive frameworks based on the order in which ideas and skills should be learned, addressing 21st century literacies requires a shift in thinking about the nature and purpose of guidance on progression. In recent years various practitioners and researchers have devised frameworks that recognise that children do not progress evenly or similarly through a series of stages, but need experiences that will support and challenge them across using a range of media. Guidance such as Bearne's (2009) approach to assessing children's production of multimodal text, Leu et al.'s (2013) ideas about online comprehension, O'Mara's (2017) ideas on game-making and Bulman's (2017) work on the moving image help to map the kinds of skills, texts and concepts that children may engage with as they work with a widening repertoire of texts. Such frameworks can provide useful support in helping teachers to reflect on the kinds of experiences that are valuable for children. While many teachers can confidently identify what a child is doing that enables them to read or write a print text, there is a need to develop a professional language to describe the same kinds of things in relation to digital media. Even when such a language has been developed (as in publications produced by the British Film Institute, or in work that has sought to expand print literacy frameworks) to include the digital (e.g. Green, 2012; Wohlwend & Buchholz, 2014) such descriptions have not always reached a wider audience. New frameworks are important in supporting teachers in thinking about the range of activities and experiences they might include in classroom provision. Otherwise, as with other areas of the curriculum with which teachers are less confident, children may find themselves repeating experiences in successive years as teachers in different year groups draw on a limited pool of known activities.

Bulman's spiral framework for reading film which we mentioned above is outlined in her book, *Children's Reading of Film and Visual Literacy in the Primary Curriculum* (2017) and it serves as a useful example. Bulman maps out skills and understandings associated with reading film, based on her analysis of children's responses to tasks and activities involving film. Her framework doesn't propose a developmental model, but rather offers support for teachers in articulating and working to build on what children know and can do. She writes:

> Although this framework could be perceived as a linear model, working through the four stages, it can be seen from the children's responses that they move around the model. [...] The way the children responded at different times to different films at a variety of stages showed that they were not constantly operating within the same stage. Depending on the challenge of the film, they would move around the framework. It was regularly observed that when reading a film they had not seen before, they needed to respond as a 'reader' – through literal reading, deduction and inference, before they could offer responses at a higher level.
>
> (Bulman, 2017: 236-237)

Through using rich examples drawn from real children's experience, Bulman identifies different aspects of reading film, linked to characterisation, plot, comprehension, genre, camera, sound, editing, colour and light, and explores how children may engage with these elements with different levels of sophistication: from literal reading, deduction and inference, through to authorial/directorial intent and wider connections. Her framework provides room for both valuing what children do and identifying directions for future activity.

Importantly, though, and this is where we return to the idea of instability introduced earlier in this section, it is worth emphasising that children will often work *across* their repertoires of linguistic, textual and cultural resources in everyday life. In schooled literacy – particularly in recent years – there has been an emphasis on isolating aspects of literacy practice, extracting literacy from the flow of everyday life as children examine a specific genre (such as persuasive writing or suspense) or rehearse specific skills (such as coding or editing). Despite this, resourceful teachers have often successfully incorporated digital literacy in their interpretation of this guidance. For instance, in a case study of children writing adventure stories, Bearne (2017) shows how one teacher used animated film and encouraged her class to experiment with presentational software in order to develop a dynamic, multimodal response to the genre-based task. Commenting on one of the texts, Bearne (p. 82) describes a 'well-structured story' with mastery of 'the conventions of narrative pace and tension by the conscious combination of words, images, sound and movement'. Unfortunately, however, as Bearne observes, none of this is recognised in current 'performance criteria' in England.

The prevalence of structured state curricula in many jurisdictions has meant that schemes of work have tended to focus on specific areas of learning activity rather than being driven by interest, topic or purpose. Learning is presented as incremental – one skill or genre is learned and then the next. While we do not argue here against focused or direct teaching, we do want to suggest that such curriculum structures, if they come to dominate, can detract from opportunities for children to draw *across* their repertoires in ways that make sense to them and for reasons that matter in the moment. In doing so, they may sideline the social and cultural dimensions of learning that are likely to matter to children whether or not they are acknowledged by their teacher. As Dyson argues:

> Whatever curricular materials and activities educators offer, deep in children's own lived worlds, these activities are renegotiated, influenced by social goals which educators might not anticipate are infused with cultural material – thematic content and literacy values.

> (Dyson, 1993: 3)

Classroom activity that allows children to develop their interests and to integrate their learning in a meaningful way is a central feature of effective education. This will involve drawing upon and developing children's resources for meaning making and extending their textual repertoire to include a variety of media. Authenticity and relevance are cornerstones of the best literacy teaching and these principles also apply to issues of e-safety that we address in the following section. In fact, e-safety is probably best seen as being part and parcel of literacy learning.

Navigating e-safety

Many readers will be familiar with the way in which online shopping sites make recommendations based on previous purchases or other browsing activity. This reminds us that any online activity is embedded within densely woven networks of other activity, driven by values, purposes and demands that may well bear little relation to our own. At a time when anything we post may be used, remixed, repurposed, the digital may feel like it brings us closer, into communities of like-minded people, but what it may be doing at the same time is bringing us into relation with – and serving the interests of those – who have very different priorities and values. Recognition of the fluidity and distributed nature of online activity comes to the fore in concerns about safeguarding. Debates about the need to protect children from cyberbullying, child abuse and hate crime, for example, have intensified in recent years. Most schools now have policies in place and there is much guidance to support this work (e.g. UK Safer Internet Centre, 2018). Most agree that e-safety needs to be addressed with sensitivity to ensure a balance between equipping children to act safely and ensuring they are still able to use the internet in ways that enrich their learning and social lives. Panics about e-safety can be counter-productive. Cranmer, Selwyn and Potter, (2009), for example, found that 7–11-year-olds' understandings of e-safety were often characterised by exaggerated fears, but also that they were less aware of the risks that were likely. It would seem that schools need to work with children and parents to understand more about their online experiences and the concerns they have in order to decide how best to respond (Hope, 2013), but also to explore how children may use these experiences in ways that are empowering to them in their everyday lives (see Chapter 9).

Summary

In this chapter we have argued for the importance of building on children's interest and experience, recognising their communication repertoire as an asset. Although much has been written about 'what today's children can do', we emphasise instead, the need for careful observation and identification of children's understandings and practices with new media, partly because these are so rich and varied. We have shown how children's communication repertoires are complex and patterned by family and community experience as well as wider influences. If these repertoires are not recognised in the classroom, disadvantage may perpetuate. Instead, cultural and linguistic resources can be converted into digital capital. Finally, we have suggested that teachers can build on children's experience of texts, and use available literacy frameworks to create rich and meaningful experiences.

QUESTIONS FOR REFLECTION

1. Think of a classroom topic or project that might provide opportunities for children to extend their communication repertoire using digital media. What practical steps could you take to draw on their digital capital? What are the opportunities and challenges associated with doing this?

2. A number of curriculum frameworks are referred to in this chapter. Which do you find most useful and why? You may wish to do further background reading on curriculum documents that you are not familiar with.

3. What is your experience of e-safety guidelines in the school context? How helpful did you (and the children) find these?

4

ACKNOWLEDGE DIVERSE
MODES AND MEDIA

Literacies have always been multimodal, but an explicit recognition of multiple modes can enable children to explore, develop and convey meanings in ways that might otherwise be overlooked. Opportunities to create using multiple modes help learners to explore ideas and possibilities in more nuanced ways, and digital media certainly make this easier. A specific knowledge of alphabetic representation and visual design are an integral part of this. However, these are not separate skills but develop in tandem alongside other modes of communication.

This chapter will:

- outline how research studies have contributed to our understanding of the key characteristics of new forms of communication

- examine how media and modality can be used to describe children's textual repertoire

- explore how teachers can support children's multimodal meaning making using a range of digital and non-digital media.

It's a rainy morning in November and Nia is putting the finishing touches to a storyboard for her *Animoto* presentation on Neptune. She's already sourced some stock images and some movie footage and Rob, her class teacher, has shown her group how short captions and still and moving images can be combined with music to good effect on *Animoto*. Hannah's short presentation will be posted on a blog shared between six other primary schools in the city. She hopes to get plenty of feedback or comments and is eager to see what other nine year-olds in the project have been up to. After school that day she sends a message from home to her friends, using the school intranet, to find out what other groups in her class were up to. They've each chosen different topics to explore the Earth and Space theme.

These children's use of *Animoto*, an online environment that allows you to upload, sequence and cloud-store video projects, builds on their home experience of media, combining with school-based work developed over several years. The finished projects will be shared online, and children from a network of schools in the area will view and comment on the work. The children in Rob's class find this project highly motivating, partly because they are able to draw on familiar formats (such as TV-style interviews, animations and documentaries) and partly because their work is stored and can be accessed remotely and watched repeatedly. These multimodal projects are more widely available than pencil-and-paper work, and can be viewed by friends and relatives as well as pupils from other schools. And because of some of the interactive features, other children can leave comments and provide feedback – this is of particular interest to Nia.

School systems are often criticised for their inherently conservative nature and teachers, too, can be characterised as being resistant to change. As we have already noted, classrooms in a number of anglophone countries have, for the last ten years or so, been dominated by a 'back-to-basics' agenda with a strong emphasis on the skills associated with print literacy. Not, one might think, particularly fertile ground for work on new media. But teachers like Rob do exist, and are an inspiration because they quietly continue to provide children with rich experiences at school – ones that value their knowledge and their cultural capital and make creative use of new forms of communication. In planning the Earth and Space work, Rob admits that the current curriculum is, in his words, 'a bit boring'. He is keen to help children to build on their communication repertoire and he is keen to capture the spirit of 'social media' both in and beyond the classroom. This involves producing meaning collectively and sharing material democratically, rather than it being handed down from a single source. But it also involves using new media and its multimodal affordances. Rob, however, doesn't describe this as a 'media project' or 'multimodal' work – although it is both of these. He is more interested in providing good learning experiences for children, ones that build on what they know and are in step with the world outside the classroom. As his children learn, so they develop their textual repertoire.

This chapter focuses on how teachers can provide opportunities for children to develop their textual repertoire in classrooms. To begin with it explores this concept of textual repertoire further, in order to understand what working with a range of media actually involves. We then move on to show how a multimodal perspective can help to develop our understanding of meaning making in new contexts.

Defining media

It is often said that we are living in a 'new media age' (Kress, 2003) or in a time of media saturation, and it certainly is the case that media have become a major preoccupation. We agonise over the possible ill-effects on children and young people of overexposure to media, advocate limits on 'screen time' (Squire, & Steinkuehler 2017) as well as the exercise of other kinds of parental control, and in society at large we are as alert to potential risks as we are to the benefits of social media. Appadurai (1996), in his analysis of late modernity, identified the role of media in globalisation, coining the term 'mediascapes' to refer to the transnational production and dissemination of information. Other commentators (such as Horst, 2008; Ito et al., 2008) follow Postman's notion of 'media ecologies' (Gencarelli, 2006) as a way of describing the ways in which we inhabit a complex media environment that is comprised of a varied and intersecting set of influences. Here we favour the idea that understanding and engaging with everyday media should underpin how we think about children's textual repertoire and how we enable them to extend that repertoire and make informed choices.

Once shorthand for mass media such as television, film and newspapers, the proliferation and diversification of media are now a key feature of public life. For example, at the time of writing, just after a General Election in the UK, there is much debate on the role of *Facebook* and *Twitter* in swaying political opinion and in mobilising the youth vote. At the same time there is rapid manoeuvring within political circles, often taking place on *WhatsApp*, and no shortage of speculation in both mainstream and social media. Thinking about media from this perspective illustrates how the adoption of mobile and digital communication has broadened the range of channels for communication that are available to us. Buckingham (2003) explains that the term media refers to the whole of this range – 'television, the cinema, video, radio, photography, advertising, newspapers and magazines, recorded music, computer games and the internet' (p. 3), and argues for a media education that has both a creative and a critical dimension. In this chapter we are concerned with the former whereas in Chapter 9 we will turn our attention to issues of criticality.

If we look more closely at the short video project described at the beginning of this chapter it becomes clear that children are showing a sophisticated understanding of the ways in which moving image communicates meaning, an understanding they have likely developed through extensive viewing (Mackey, 2017). However, their film also incorporates understandings about oral and written language as well as diagrammatic representation. Indeed, one of the characteristics of new media and screen-based communication in general is the way in which they combine different meaning-making systems. In film, for example, the use of music or ambient sound may often go unnoticed, but it is, of course, an integral part of the experience, setting the mood or atmosphere to particular scenes. This interweaving of meaning making systems is what is referred to as multimodality, the topic to which we turn our attention to now. So, while media is used to refer to channels of communication, multimodality is concerned with describing or explaining how that communication works and how meaning is constructed or designed within those various media.

Exploring multimodality

Much of the current educational interest in multimodality stems from the influential work of Gunther Kress who has developed ideas about social semiotics and used them to comment on the new technologies of information and communication. Kress (2003) suggests that we are moving (or have moved) from an era in which the page is replaced by the screen as the dominant site for communication. This shift includes a move away from the dominance of alphabetic literacy to a situation, or landscape of communication, which includes still and moving image, spoken language and other modes. In Kress's work '*Mode* is the name for a culturally and socially fashioned resource for representation and communication' (Kress, 2003: 45). In this key work he gives speech, dance, music and image as examples of different modes. Here, of course, we might think of Nia's Neptune Animoto or recall the rise of short-form video. Kress's idea is that this sort of meaning making is multimodal, since it conveys meaning through a combination of different modes. From this point of view, something like a video could be seen as an orchestration or ensemble of modes.

This multimodal perspective has been applied in a number of different contexts, such as the analysis of children's writing and drawing (QCA, 2004, 2005), game-based machinima video (Merchant, 2013a) as well as classroom interaction (Taylor, 2012, 2014), and has been put to good use by linguists and educators. The idea that children should learn about the affordances of different modes, make design choices in combining modes and be assessed in ways that take account of their multimodal skills has been influential in the development of the multiliteracies movement (Cope & Kalantzis, 2000), and subsequently in various state and national curriculum initiatives. Multimodality ushers in a new theory of meaning – and it is one that has sometimes proved problematic in debates about literacy. Some academics and practitioners are happy that the term literacy is expanded to embrace all forms of meaning making, including all modes and combinations of modes, whereas others are keen to maintain the link between literacy and lettered representation even if they are also committed to media education (see Merchant, 2007a).

Important though such debates may be, it seems more important to us that curricular provision should include plenty of opportunities for using and producing multimodal texts through a range of media. Of course, this should not take place at the expense of learning reading and writing as they are traditionally conceived. In fact, we need to acknowledge that human communication is more diverse and more complex than it once was, and that even reading and writing are subject to change (see Chapter 2). This not only refers to the changing conventions of alphabetic literacies and to innovations like the development and use of emojis, but also to technological developments that allow us to 'read' material such as audio books and 'write' with sophisticated voice recognition software. Nevertheless, as Brandt's work demonstrates so well, we are now writing more than we have ever done before in history (Brandt, 2015). So while we argue for developing children's textual repertoire, this repertoire must include learning the skills and techniques of lettered representation.

Diverse modes and media in the classroom

Acknowledging the changing nature of communication has implications for how we plan and teach in the classroom. Inevitably this extends across subjects and cannot be the sole responsibility of literacy or English. It therefore requires a significant change in how we think about representing meaning in learning and teaching. A useful way of approaching such a change of emphasis is to think about mapping the purposes of different learning tasks to particular media. Here we adapt a familiar model for thinking about writing – one that considers purpose, audience and form. By expanding the category of form we are able to illustrate the sort of diversity in media and mode that we have been referring to in this chapter. Table 4.1 gives some examples of how this mapping might work and how a consideration of different purposes and audiences connects with the idea of textual repertoire (media and modes).

Table 4.1 Mapping textual repertoire through a consideration of purpose and audience

Purpose	Audience	Media	Modes
Informing	Children in a partner school	Online platform (e.g. a blog)	Writing Still image
Interacting	A professional storyteller	*Twitter* and *Skype*	Writing Speech
Imagining	Other children in the class	Virtual world or sandbox game (e.g. *Minecraft*)	Moving image Writing
Presenting	Other children in the school	Presentational software (e.g. *Animoto*)	Still image
Narrating	Other children/adults	E-book	Still image Speech Writing

To illustrate this further, we draw on the research of Rowe and Miller (2017), working in a multilingual context in the US, who were interested in developing e-book composition in the early years. As we know there is a range of apps on the market that provide templates for children to create their own e-books by adding audio and visual content alongside written text (Kucirkova et al., 2013). Rowe and Miller (2017) explored what happened when two groups of young bilingual children (4- and 7-year-olds) made their own e-books using these resources. Initially the two groups used digital cameras to take photographs of what interested them at home and at school. As these photographs travelled between the two sites they generated plenty of interest and discussion about the similarities and differences in children's experience. The children were then supported in composing multilingual e-books using the app *Book Creator* and importing their images. They later shared these e-books with their peers on a large screen at school. The project provided a rich opportunity for making their language capabilities and cultural experiences visible (Rowe and Miller, 2017), but also raised questions for the authors about how such projects sit within wider educational provision. Rowe and Miller found, for example, that speakers of some minority languages (such as Somali and Arabic) did not engage as much as Spanish speakers in creating voice recordings. They only started to do so when other opportunities for valuing and using these languages were introduced into the classroom. Despite this finding, the work shows the benefits of building on children's cultural capital (see Chapter 2). In this case the children's knowledge of heritage languages was brought to the fore alongside their growing familiarity with new technology.

In another project – this time based in New South Wales, Australia – Simpson and Walsh (2017) tracked children's textual repertoire while they were engaged in the process of creating a radio segment about the health risks associated with junk food. Students used iPads to access and read fast-food facts and made handwritten notes as they developed their ideas. They used *GarageBand* to produce their radio feature and then presented it to peers, later discussing the content in video interviews. Simpson and Walsh describe the layers of meaning that were involved as each successive text became part of the development of the next. The researchers explored the interplay of semiotic systems that unfold when children draw on a variety of modes on screen and in print in this way, tracing the movement between individual, collaborative and communal activity. They also illustrate how digital and non-digital resources interweave during the process of composition and in doing this suggest that the layering of different textual engagements may be supportive of children's in-depth conceptual understanding. They argue that it is important not only to understand how modes interact at the textual level but also how modes interact at the contextual level, in this case in a classroom-based project in which tablets were used to explore multimodal design – another approach to extending children's textual repertoire.

'Old' media and 'new' media

As we have already suggested, the concept of textual repertoire emphasises the importance of working with the full range of meaning-making tools and this must, by definition, include more traditional forms of representation, as the previous example illustrates. So far we have used the term new media as shorthand for digital resources, but this is not a way of suggesting that the new is in some way better than the old. We argue instead that different meaning-making tools have different roles to play and different strengths too, and this is related to both their potential (or affordance) and their availability. It could well be argued that with the development of a broader range of meaning-making resources we arrive at a heightened awareness of the affordances of different modes and media. Indeed, some authors have developed the idea that an understanding of affordances underpins the design choices that are now central to textual composition (e.g. Cope & Kalantzis, 2000).

Kress uses the term 'affordance' as a way of describing the meaning-making potential and limitations of different modes. Contrasting a graphic 'No Smoking' sign with a printed no smoking policy, Kress (2003: 52) shows how the first effectively and economically conveys its message, whereas the second fulfils a very different set of purposes. Thinking about affordances in this way is helpful in informing classroom decisions about the use of different media and modes, and what they can offer in terms of learning and teaching. The perspective is particularly relevant to discussions about digital literacy. However, classroom life is often constrained by the availability of resources. Not all classrooms may be as generously equipped with the hardware described above – and even where laptops and tablets are available a whole host of challenges can intervene including the number of devices that actually work or have the right software installed and so on.

In light of this we turn now to examples of ways in which teachers and researchers have found creative methods of engaging with new media in contexts that are not favourably resourced. In our own work we engaged in discussions with Year 6 children about their knowledge and use of mobile phones and challenged them with the task of designing and marketing a new kind of phone. In preparation the children looked at mobile phone advertisements and considered them in terms of their multimodal design, focusing on the language features and use of visual images. Paired work generated ideas about new design features, based on children's existing knowledge of mobile phones. Subsequently, their independent work involved them in producing rough sketches of a new phone, listing its design features and making a plan for a poster. Their designs included a shockproof phone that would not be damaged when dropped as well as a waterproof model – the swim-phone (see QCA, 2004).

In another project, in a pre-primary school in the Finnish city of Oulu, teachers were keen to explore and discuss 6-year-old children's knowledge of and interest in digital games. Children were encouraged to use existing classroom materials to design and draw 'the best game in the world'. Often these newly designed imaginary games incorporated and developed the features of already existing videogames. Some children generated completely novel ideas whereas others thought that their favourite games were already perfect and did not want to change anything. The project was further developed by designing and constructing a board game from recycled materials. This work was done by groups of children with an interest in the same kind of games – a creative and social project in its own right. Here children were able to discuss and reflect on new media and design processes in a productive way using the materials at hand (see Salomaa & Mertala, forthcoming, for further discussion).

Finally, another obstacle that is sometimes encountered occurs in contexts in which curriculum guidance does not explicitly refer to the use of new media, or when print literacy skills are privileged through the emphasis given to them by high-stakes testing. There are, however, many examples of work in which educators have demonstrated how curriculum objectives can be met through the use of new media. We conclude by looking at the work of Wohlwend and Buchholz who contextualise their work by explaining that:

> We are living in a digital era when we finally have sophisticated and user-friendly technologies that are just right for little fingers to operate and to easily capture children's play texts. Specifically, touchscreens on phones and tablets are mobile and responsive, with filmmaking apps that are simple and intuitive. These new tools seem designed for early-childhood teachers to use with their students. To be clear, we do not intend to invoke an old/new binary and either/or choice, often constructed around print and digital tools. Rather, we follow the children's lead to see how they are using and making texts with *all* the multiple resources they find around them, from paper and pencil to tape and popsicle sticks to cameras and digital video.
>
> (Wohlwend & Buchholz, 2014: 33)

The project that they document involved creating large puppets out of popsicle sticks, developing plotlines through play and then filming particular play sequences (see Chapter 8). Wohlwend and Buchholz argue that the introduction of cameras drew on children's understanding and experience of media while at the same time prompting them to generate rich multi-modal narratives. Throughout this work they demonstrate how this activity addresses conventional curriculum requirements associated with narrative writing that appear as benchmarks in the mandated curriculum. At the same time the work moved beyond these requirements to develop new media literacies.

Summary

In this chapter we have considered how scholarship on media and multimodality has enriched our understanding of new literacies. Providing a brief introduction to these areas has set the scene for an exploration of how these ideas have informed innovative practice in classrooms. Throughout this chapter we have drawn attention to the importance of textual repertoire. To participate in social, cultural and political life now requires a wide repertoire of communication skills, and a creative and critical approach to this is rapidly becoming a necessity. Children's current and future communication needs are unlikely to be met through a curriculum that simply focuses on print literacy. Moreover, such a curriculum will be out of step with everyday life and runs the danger of being seen as irrelevant. The examples we have included here suggest that it is possible to provide creative and engaging activity whatever the circumstances and that children's learning can be enriched through the use of diverse modes and media.

••

QUESTIONS FOR REFLECTION

1. Thinking of a classroom you are familiar with, consider the resources that are available for working in the sorts of ways outlined in this chapter. How might you extend the communication repertoire of children in this class using these resources?

2. What are the challenges of including print and digital literacies in the classroom and how might these be overcome?

••

5

RECOGNISE THE AFFECTIVE, EMBODIED AND MATERIAL DIMENSIONS OF MEANING MAKING

The meanings we make are inflected by what we feel, what has just happened and who we are with, as well as how we are positioned by the people and things around us. The immediate environment, resources, personal and shared histories therefore all play a part in what children do with digital media. Literacy provision therefore needs to take account of affective, embodied and material dimensions of communicative practice.

This chapter will:

- explore the role of affect in using and making digital media
- consider the significance of children being together with each other on- and off-screen
- consider the creative and expressive opportunities that are generated when children follow what matters to them in the moment.

Lewis and Joshua are using *Scratch* to create a game which involves stopping a sausage pie from being eaten by a shark. They sketch out their idea on paper and then start to make the game. They begin by searching for a sprite to insert. Having found one, they insert the simple coding that will make it bounce up and down repeatedly. They seem to take turns automatically. Lewis leans forward and takes control of the keyboard for a while, and then leans back, angling the laptop towards Joshua for him to take over.

(Continued)

(Continued)

Once they've finished inserting the bouncy sprite they try it out a few times, pressing the key to make it bounce up and down, pointing at it and laughing. Next they google 'sausage pie with a shark eating it'. They're not happy with the first set of images that Google presents and Joshua rethinks – 'I know, we'll need a cartoon one.' Their revised search for 'cartoon pie with sausages in it' generates a range of more suitable images and they burst out laughing, holding the laptop up and rotating it round for others working at their table to see. They scroll through the images, reviewing some, passing quickly over others. Eventually they select one and import it to their game. They giggle at the sight of the cartoon sausage on the screen and call out to others nearby who momentarily gather round their laptop to see it, giggling too with appreciation then dispersing again.

Lewis and Joshua approach the task of making their game with apparent confidence, searching for images to use and gradually bringing their ideas to fruition. In doing so they meet the lesson objectives, derived from the Computing curriculum they are following (DfE, 2013), which require them to be able to code a series of actions on screen. But somehow, that straightforward description manages to conceal other important dimensions of their classroom experience – there are other things going on here too. Their choice of sprites, images and actions all demonstrate a rather playful approach to game-making. They are making a game to amuse themselves and their friends, and it is not just the finished game that they're pleased with – they also have fun as they do so. Playing in this way, Lewis and Joshua have transformed the game-making into something more than a technical exercise, and this is why we include it here in a book on digital media (as opposed to one on computing). It's not just about a set of codes but it's a game designed to entertain and amuse, and the choice of sprites and speed of bounce all matter because of this. The *Scratch* game-making example may seem rather trivial, but it illustrates how children weave themselves, their stories, their humour and their preferences into school activities, and how whatever they do always happens in relation to the people and things that are there with them in the moment.

As Joshua and Lewis worked together there was none of the dialogue we might expect to see in negotiating turn-taking – 'your go' perhaps, or 'when's it my turn?'– and very little discussion about what they were actually going to do. They simply seemed to watch what the other was doing and then take over where he had left off. This improvisational approach is something we explore further in Chapter 6, and in Chapter 10 we consider how digital environments generate rich possibilities for collaboration on- and off-screen. But in this chapter we are interested in a different aspect of this collaborative production. We explore how the very experience of *being together* seems to be important in keeping up the momentum, for what children do and the kinds of meanings that they make.

So what matters?

As educators it's easy to justify the integration of digital media in order to promote children's future economic success, or their active and safe participation in a digitally mediated world. However, for children in classrooms, the things that matter may be much more immediate and ephemeral: the excitement of playing with the possibilities of a new digital environment, for example, the hilarity as they encounter something they find absurd, or the gentle rhythms of generating stuff on-screen.

Recently literacy researchers have been thinking about the *affective* dimension of literacy practices (see Leander & Ehret, 2018). Definitions of affect vary, but the definition most relevant to what we discuss in this chapter is influenced by the work of Massumi (2002) and developed from the ideas of philosophers Deleuze and Guattari (1987). Affect, as we refer to it here, is the feeling generated as people and things meet up in the moment. Rather than thinking about emotions – the feelings experienced and described by individuals – affect refers to the feeling generated as people and things come into *relation* or *assemble*. Affect may be experienced differently by different individuals, but the feeling is generated among – or in between – those present. This sounds rather abstract, but many teachers will be familiar with the feeling that a lesson or activity 'went well', a lesson which perhaps fell flat when they tried to repeat it another time – somehow things just didn't assemble in the same way as they had done before.

There is *always* affect as people and things *always* meet up in any moment, although this may be punctuated by moments of 'affective intensities' and these moments may well be those that spur creativity (Hollett & Ehret, 2015) – the appearance of the bouncing sprite in the episode above might well have been one of these. Thinking about something as ephemeral and elusive as affect is tricky, but it can highlight aspects of children's meaning making that might otherwise escape our notice. As we explore further in Chapter 6, creativity is emergent by nature and ideas often take off through improvisations based on what matters in the moment. Such moments clearly cannot be planned for but their significance does need to be acknowledged. As Leander writes:

> This is the quality of discussions that break into laughter or performances, of story readings that break into life story-tellings and paintings – anywhere there is a break that cannot be anticipated in a priori rationales for why we will spend an hour or day in school. If the day's

activity could readily be recorded for the student who was absent, then it's likely that nothing emergent happened.

(Boldt, Lewis & Leander, 2015: 435–6)

Daniels (2017), for example, explores how 4- and 5-year-olds played with and around a series of apps made available to them in an early years classroom. She describes how the children improvised with the apps, sometimes using them in ways that were different from the uses intended (or expressed) by app designers. Playing a game that involved manoeuvring a robot through a maze, one boy, for example, repeatedly crashed the robot into the sides, seemingly because he delighted in the noise it made and the chance it gave him to have another go. In doing so, he recruited the boy next to him as his audience, laughing out loud with him as the app beeped and beeped. Daniels found that children were more creative when using apps that were open-ended, or when they found new ways of playing with more narrowly focused apps:

> [I]t often appeared that, when engaging with apps with linear or closed content, children seemed to work quietly and individually, and shifted quite quickly from one app to another. In other episodes, where the content of apps was not linked to specific and discrete literacy skills, or was more open ended, children did appear to access them differently. Collaborative interaction around such apps offered an opportunity for creative engagement as the children learned to control them, explore their possibilities and infuse such activity with meanings significant to their lives and interests. In this way, the apps became a site for engagement amongst peers where friendships, relationships and shared interests emerged.

(Daniels, 2017: 216)

Thinking about affect prompts us to think about digital media-making in terms of what happens as children, teachers and things assemble in classrooms, and about the opportunities that might be generated or curtailed as things assemble differently from moment to moment. Rather than focusing on what is on-screen (or in children's heads), we might focus instead on digital media-making as part of an ongoing flow of activity, with texts taking shape as part of this flow rather than as endpoints. These kinds of movements are often very apparent when children play in the playground or at home. One activity morphs into another and objects get taken up and discarded as the play unfolds (see also Chapter 6). While classroom activity is often ostensibly about 'making progress' as captured through specific learning objectives or outcomes, for children it is likely to be about much more.

If we are to help generate opportunities in which children are driven to experiment and explore, then it's important to consider how and why one activity leads to another, and to be aware of the role of affect.

Being together

This discussion of affect has implications for thinking about how we support children as they collaborate with one another. Although much attention has been given to classroom collaboration, from the early work of researchers like Barnes (1976) to more recent contributions (such as Littleton & Mercer, 2013), most of this has focused on collaborative talk. This research exploring the quality of children's dialogue has been very influential in primary education: Alexander's work on dialogic teaching, for example, and Mercer's recommendations for talk to support 'thinking together' continue to inform pedagogy in many schools. However, a focus on affect – and the different ways in which people and things assemble – raises other kinds of questions about what happens as children are together in classrooms. It is not just what children say but the proximity of bodies, the heat and humidity of the classroom, the arrangement of desks and so on that will matter, along with prior experiences of doing and being in relation to other bodies and things (Burnett, 2015a, 2015b). These complex inter-weavings play into what happens in any moment.

In one classroom, for example, Year 6 children used an open-source videogame, *Proteus*, as the starting point for some creative writing. *Proteus* is a lyrical game in which players explore a magical natural world of forests, lakes and dark skies. While in some senses the world is produced through their play – it is the action of moving through the world that generates new places – players can't change the features of the world or create new things themselves as they might do in *Minecraft*. *Proteus* seems to offer much as a stimulus for descriptive writing, and indeed this class eventually produced some compelling descriptions of the virtual world they had explored. At one point during the lesson, though, two boys – Josh and Luke – found another way of playing. By accident they discovered that pressing the 'escape' button caused them to be ejected from the world and they had to restart the time-consuming process of loading the game. Seeing an opportunity, they shouted across to other children: 'Press escape and you'll find yourself in a magical world.' As others did so – and were duly ejected – the two boys collapsed in laughter and the joke built as more and more children fell for the trick. Not everyone was caught up in this, however. Lizzy, sitting near the boys, moved away from the raucous group and settled by a bookcase. There she proceeded to write alone, engaging with the writing task the teacher had set (see Burnett, 2015b, for more detail).

This episode illustrates how bodies and things can assemble differently from moment to moment and how these different 'assemblings' generate different kinds of possibilities. Groupings of children, for example, are not fixed but fluid, children – and things – get positioned differently from moment to moment, and they may experience these fluctuations differently, with new possibilities opening up or being curtailed as they get positioned in different ways.

Activity and things

In some recent writing on literacies much is made of the different meanings of the word *matter*. So far we have used it in the sense of what is important – and particularly what is important or what matters to children. But the word is also used to draw attention to physical matter – the *things* that are also part of the assemblings we have been referring to above. This includes the material objects in place – the tables, chairs, bookshelves, paper, iPads and so on – as well as environmental features such as the shape and feel of a classroom or corridor. Hollett and Ehret (2017), for example, refer to the way in which the echoes from a stairwell and the 'feel' of a school auditorium helped to produce a distinctive atmosphere, giving the video-making project they were observing its unique texture. Researchers have also explored the materiality of technology, adding another dimension to a substantial body of work on digital literacy that has tended to focus on what happens on-screen in human–machine interactions (see, for example, Davies & Merchant, 2009).

In a study focusing on young children and iPad story-apps, attention was given to the materiality of the iPads themselves (Merchant, 2015b). Initially, video data were analysed to create a typology of the ways in which the children handled these tablet devices. This revealed the variety of ways that children held, steadied and worked with iPads.

Table 5.1 shows this typology, which draws our attention to the work of the hands in using mobile touchscreen technology. The typology was subsequently combined with a microanalysis of story-sharing, derived from the work of Taylor (2010). Looking in this way at the materiality of the technology and the ways in which the size, weight and heft of the tablet device along with its specific operative functions *invited* certain kinds of bodily responses is an important perspective. But at the same time it was clear that these characteristics played into the distinctive ways in which meanings were made, how the apps were experienced, how the children navigated their ways through the texts, as well as how texts were then shared. In this sense then, we could say that technologies are active in helping to shape both the physical and social actions and interactions of users through their material and technological affordances.

Table 5.1   Hand movements used in the iPad study

1. Stabilising movements
Holding *using one or both hands to support the tablet (as one might hold a tray).*
Holding and resting *as above but using legs/knees for additional support (often only one hand is used).*
2. Control movements
General tapping *using three or four fingers in a slapping motion (commonly used by the young children).*
Precision tapping *using the forefinger (like the pointing gesture) or with the hand palm downwards slightly lowering one of the first three fingers so that it activates the screen.*
Swiping *hand palm downward using one or more fingers to drag across the screen while maintaining contact.*
Thumb pressing *using the thumb to tap, swipe or operate the home button.*
3. Deictic movements
Pointing, nodding and other gestures – *directing attention to the iPad, the screen or visual items framed by the screen.*

(Merchant, 2015b)

Of course, things don't always run smoothly and predictably. As we have shown in the earlier sections of this chapter, bodies and things can assemble in all sorts of ways. There is useful description of this in the work of Hollett and Ehret which we referred to above.

> The iPad app momentarily locks up, and the iPad's materiality asserts itself into the production of frustrating feelings that become contagious, that become a feeling in the air, a feeling that a teacher might mobilize herself in response to before saying to herself, 'these students are getting off track'; the iPad restarts itself and allows the flow of production to continue; teachers and students feel again an enthusiasm for the new media projects developing.
>
> *(Hollett & Ehret, 2017: 239–240)*

In classrooms, bodies and things assemble in ways that are not expected, and many of these may well be ignored or simply not noticed by busy teachers. During one classroom study, for example, children were observed using iPads in all kinds of ways: not just in relation to use of different apps – as cameras, archives, word processors, etc. – but also in relation to their size and shape – as trays, walls, surfaces and so on (Burnett, 2017). And returning to the video footage from which he identified the categories of hand movements described above, Merchant (2017) noted other kinds of movements of bodies and things that happened alongside those closely related to storysharing: dangling feet, fiddling with socks, untied shoelaces, children walking away or gazing into the video camera. What matters then may well coincide with teachers' learning aims, or may not. It may unfold in expected ways, throwing up unexpected opportunities for meaning-making that teachers may want to encourage, or signalling a loss of interest or distress that might prompt a change of direction. Moreover, in a detailed analysis of 4- to 5-year-olds' activity in an early years classroom, Daniels (2016) indicates how children's activities that may well seem incidental to classroom tasks often involve intense interest that in turn generates meaning making.

In early years settings in many countries, practitioners are used to following children's interests in supporting children's learning. In primary schools, particularly where testing regimes exist which are linked to school accountability, such flexibility may be harder to accommodate. Nevertheless, as we explore in Chapter 6, allowing time, space and resources for improvisation can generate creativity. Paying attention to the different ways in which bodies and things interact in classrooms can alert teachers to what matters to children from moment to moment. This in turn can indicate possibilities for making meaning that might be encouraged, as well as possible barriers or injustices that children might need support or encouragement to overcome.

Summary

In this chapter we have explored the role of affect in meaning making. We have defined affect as the feeling generated as people and things meet up in the moment. We have described how the affective dimension of being together in classrooms matters to what children do with digital media, and suggested that this 'being together' involves not just children and teachers, but children and the things they encounter, including digital devices and other resources, furniture and so on. Supporting children to use digital media in collaborative, creative and critical ways, therefore, involves being sensitive to how this affective dimension may be empowering or disempowering to individuals and groups.

QUESTIONS FOR REFLECTION

1. Reflect on a recent 'literacy event' in which you were involved? How do you think affect played into this? How did this change (e.g. intensify) from moment to moment? And why do think this might have been the case?

2. Think about a classroom that you know well. What does the arrangement of furniture and resources suggest about what is valued in this classroom? Is children's use of resources regulated in any way? How do children arrange themselves in relation to the furniture and resources? How far is this as you might expect? What does this suggest about how they approach literacy in school?

3. What do you notice about the way children interact with other children and with things around them? What does this suggest about what matters to them? What does this mean for how you understand what matters in classroom literacy provision?

6

ENCOURAGE IMPROVISATION AND EXPERIMENTATION

Although intentional design and production are important aspects of multimodal work, creative engagement is often unplanned and emergent in nature. Facilitating this sort of experimentation is based on an understanding of how meaning is made in the moment which may, or may not, result in a finished product.

This chapter will:

- expand on the importance of recognising emergent dimensions of meaning-making

- introduce ways in which improvisation and experimentation can be encouraged

- explore the importance of encouraging children to draw from across their repertoires of communication practice.

Fran's fingers are pressed onto the keyboard so that her avatar flies high and fast over the town. She's searching for pigs.

Sophie, next to Fran, faces her own screen. Her avatar is on the ground at the foot of a skyscraper. Pink rectangular blocks are appearing rapidly in front of it.

Sophie points at her screen and calls, 'Fran'. When Fran doesn't respond, she points at Fran's screen, indicating one of the pink blocks. Fran leans forward and recognises the pink blocks for what they are in *Minecraft* – 'pigs!'

Sophie leans back in her chair, saying to Fran, 'which you don't know ... is that I spawned them'.

Fran doesn't appear to be listening; she's intent on moving her avatar closer to the pigs and her eyes are fixed on the screen. When she's moved it to where she wants, she jumps onto a pig and starts riding.

(Continued)

(Continued)

Fran leans back and clenches both fists in triumph – 'I'm on top of a pig'. Sophie turns to Fran again, and repeats, 'what you don't know is that I spawned them'.

This time, Fran seems to hear. She glances at Sophie, then turns back at her screen and starts typing in the chatscreen – 'Hallelujah'. She points at the word on her screen then, when Sophie doesn't look, reaches across her friend and points at the chatscreen on Sophie's laptop, indicating what she just wrote. She smiles and looks back at her own screen chanting, 'Pig, pig, pig, pig, pig, pig, pig, pig'. She continues riding.

Sophie turns back to her screen, reads the comment and starts typing herself. Her words appear on the chatscreen in front of her, but I don't catch them this time. I do though, see her reach across Fran and point across at what she has just written, which is now appearing on Fran's chatscreen. Fran turns back to her screen and starts typing a new entry.

(Abridged from Burnett, forthcoming)

This 60-second episode happened during a lunchtime Minecraft Club, led by Chris Bailey, at that time a teacher in the school, during which 10–11-year-olds were invited to build a community called Bradborough using *MinecraftEdu* (Burnett & Bailey, 2014). The children built whatever they liked: a statue, a theatre, a library, a hotel, a rollercoaster, high-rise buildings, small cottages, and so on (see Figure 6.1). Sometimes they arrived at Minecraft Club with very clear plans of what to build, and sometimes they sustained projects over a series of weeks. However, often they simply started building and improvised from there; repeated clicking and selection led to the intensely rapid production of blocks or digging of cavernous pits. Choices about colour, tools and materials were made quickly and rarely discussed. Ideas seemed to be generated through the momentum of building, and design was playful not planned. As one girl commented, 'basically you just start doing something and then it looks like something else and suddenly you get an idea of something and end up doing something by accident.'

In the example above, Fran and Sophie were sitting next to each other in class playing in Bradborough on separate laptops. Sophie was working on a squid aquarium while Fran was looking for pigs to ride. Fran had ridden pigs before but on this occasion she could not find any until Sophie came to her rescue and generated some for her. Fran and Sophie both had ideas about what they wanted to do – ride pigs or build an aquarium – but in many ways what they did wasn't planned at all: it unfolded *as they played*. Sophie interrupted her own play to help Fran out when she saw she was upset, the aquarium took shape as Sophie placed each brick on

Figure 6.1   Building the Minecraft Club Town

the last and saw (and maybe felt) what was possible and Sophie started using the chatscreen once Fran did. None of these actions were discussed. Fran and Sophie responded in the moment to what appeared on screen and to what the other did, and their play headed off in different directions as they did so. This very ordinary episode is the kind of virtual play that many children engage in, and in other chapters of this book we explore different dimensions of what happens as children play together in this way. In this chapter we focus on the *improvisational* quality of what children do, and in the following chapter we explore the role of playfulness in teaching, of responding to what children do and of 'going with the flow'.

Improvisation has long been associated with creativity, but as many educators and scholars know, the notion of creativity itself is complex and contested (Grainger, Goouch & Lambirth, 2005). Nevertheless, working and playing together – or creating something – often has an improvisational character, particularly when the process of working collaboratively becomes more than the sum of its parts, one thing leads to another and something new or unexpected arises. This is a recurrent theme in the study of new media. Lankshear and Knobel (2011: 42) illustrate the phenomenon in their exploration of remixing. Using the 'Iraqi shoe toss meme' as an example, they show how a short news media clip was distributed, taken up, and reworked to build new meanings. Although this is an example of an online practice, in which participants were probably not co-present, Fran and Sophie are engaged in a similar process of taking up ideas, pushing them in new directions, actively producing meanings.

We can also see this at work in more established literacy practices. Setting out to write something – like a chapter for this book, for example – is always a slightly alarming prospect. You know broadly what it is you want to write and writing it seems important, but you're never quite sure what it's going to look like in the end. Even when you do have a well-worked plan, things often shift a little as you start to write – an idea emerges and you head off in an unexpected direction, often ending up with something quite different from what you had initially had in mind. It's as if the act of writing, whether on screen or on paper, somehow itself generates new ideas and fresh directions, and things fall out onto the page or screen in unexpected ways. Writing, then, isn't simply about writing down what you want to say: the act of writing itself generates new ideas, maybe because it slows you down, maybe because starting to juxtapose words, sentences, paragraphs – as you do when you write – helps you see things in ways that you hadn't before. And new ideas, or new ways of saying things, are sometimes produced in the process – they sometimes seem simply to emerge. St Pierre sums up this experience when she writes:

> After many years of writing, I have come to believe in writing, to trust that sometimes, not all the time, but sometimes when I'm plodding along, putting one word after another after another [...] words write themselves and then close right up on themselves like an egg, and I find I've written something I couldn't have thought by thinking alone. I believe in those inconspicuous, monumental events of writing when words appear together differently – such a simple thing – and worlds open up.

> (St Pierre, 2014: 378)

So improvisation isn't new; it isn't just a feature of digital environments. But we would suggest that improvisation comes to the fore when we start thinking about how we make meaning with new media. Reflect for a moment on what you do when you go online. Even with the most straightforward of tasks – booking a holiday, for example – you might have a clear idea of a particular website to visit, but then head off in unanticipated directions as you follow up leads, check things out, or get inspired to do something quite different from what you had originally planned. And if you're creating something – even something as mundane as a *PowerPoint* presentation – it sometimes takes shape in unexpected ways as you start playing around with font, colour, images, order and so on. Working and playing on screen means you can move quickly between different apps and modes, and rapidly access multiple resources, which may fit with what you want to say, or may lead you in unexpected directions. Inserting an image, heading off to the internet to search for information or inspiration, or emailing or chatting with a friend can generate all kinds of other avenues and possibilities.

Of course, as we improvise, we're drawing on our prior experience of doing similar things – of the kinds of words that follow other words, or how our fingers press out text from a keyboard, or what might be signified by a particular sweep of a line or splash of colour. But what is also interesting is how it often feels as if ideas or new directions are *just happening*, as if what we are doing takes on a life of its own, and that often what emerges is therefore sometimes unexpected.

Making space for improvisation

Dan Power, Wil Baker and Adam Daly worked to develop a cross-school project, *The Street*, which allowed them to experiment with different conceptions of literacy. Wil and Dan were working with a Year 5 class while Adam was working with a Year 3 class and this meant that their priorities in literacy were different. As a starting point they played a sound clip to each of their classes and invited the children to respond. The children generated different kinds of responses: written responses, drawings and maps. Responses were posted online (each class used existing blogging software hosted by *Kidblog*) and viewed and sometimes responded to what had been posted. During this process various stories started to take shape, stories that weren't planned – or even owned – by either class, but that emerged as the children took up and worked with what others had posted (Monkhouse et al., 2017).

An idea took hold when one of the Year 3 children posted a description of someone 'snatching birds out of the sky' (birds could be heard on the initial sound clip and appeared in some of the Year 3's drawings). The Year 5 class seized on this idea, building the birdsnatcher into their own stories and naming him Tom O'Brien. Ideas were posted back on the blog, and together the classes built up a backstory that explained Tom O'Brien's crime, which was reported on news reports written and filmed by the Year 5 children. The teachers here gave ownership back to the children, and noted that as they did this some of the children surprised them. One child, for example, who lacked confidence in literacy lessons was highly motivated by the project and a key player in the production of a news report, and Adam noted that once his Year 3 children had the Year 5 group in mind, their writing took on a different quality: they wrote about different things, tailoring their subject matter to what they saw as the interests of an older age group, and paid more attention to some of the linguistic features that Adam had been encouraging them to focus on in literacy lessons. With some careful attention to detail and some pedagogical ingenuity the three teachers were able map this work on to curricular programmes of study, convincing school managers of the importance of their approach (see Monkhouse et al., 2017) and providing children with a range of ways of developing their communication repertoire.

In another project, Angela Colvert worked with her Year 6 class to design an alternate reality game (ARG) to be played by Year 5 children at the school (Colvert, 2012). ARGs take the form of a quest, blending together online and offline resources: ARG designers seed a series of clues that players draw on to solve problems and complete challenges. Colvert invited her class to create an ARG based on a class novel, Phillip Ridley's *The Mighty Fizz Chiller*. The Year 6 children drew on multiple media to engage in what Jenkins calls 'transmedia storytelling' (Jenkins et al., 2006), developing a series of texts – videos, maps, websites and so on – that the younger children could access online and use as clues to solve the mystery. Sometimes the Year 6 children found that the Year 5s headed off in a direction they thought was misleading, and so they had to create new clues to post on the website to help guide them back on track. Again the Year 6 children had to improvise in order to respond to the questions and conclusions Year 5 children arrived at through play.

The above examples suggest the power and potential of improvisation and experimentation in literacy provision. Interestingly, they involve the co-construction of imaginary worlds, albeit with different degrees of guidance or direction.

Writing, composing, producing

As we noted above, curriculum guidance on literacy often overlooks the importance – and complexity – of composition. When composing does come to the fore, it can easily be reduced to a particular teaching approach. So, despite the undoubted strengths of Graves' 'writing workshops' (Graves, 1983), Paley's play-based 'story-telling curriculum' (see Cooper, 2005) and post-Hallidayan 'genre teaching' (DfEE, 1998), describing learning outcomes is a challenge, not least because what we are dealing with is in essence a process or an experience. Describing these experiences, no matter how beneficial they may be, tends to elude education systems that prioritise quantifiable outcomes. Yet as Dyson suggests:

> [C]hildren enter schools with words and symbols indexing their prior travels on Bakhtin's voice-strewn landscape, that is in families, churches, sidewalks and playgrounds, neighbourhoods, radio waves and screens of all kinds. [...] Children must stretch familiar experiences from their communicative experiences if they are to participate meaningfully in the literacy practices of the school.
>
> *(Dyson, 2001: 13)*

This is a powerful statement about the importance of building on experience in early learning through drawing on children's cultural capital and their engagement in a range of communicative practices. Dyson goes on to illustrate how children actively incorporate and recontextualise these communicative practices in their early writing – but of course this all depends on sensitive teaching and an ethos that allows and encourages a variety of

kinds of meaning making. An overemphasis on literacy skills and decontex-
tualised exercises can squeeze out these possibilities.

The idea that children are *active* meaning makers is often claimed by
literacy educators and researchers (Wells, 1987), and this, in itself, is perhaps sufficient to justify the importance of promoting different kinds of
composing in classrooms – whether those acts of composition are oral, written or visual, in whatever multimodal combination. In the literature on
media studies there have been parallel moves to incorporate 'production'
alongside critical consumption, suggesting similarities with the writing–
reading relationship (Buckingham, 2003). In fact, some commentators
have observed how the two processes overlap in our participation with new
media (Burbules, 1997). One could imagine a continuum between navigating, liking and following, to curating and commenting, and producing new
content. Each of these stages involves active meaning making and varying
degrees of composition.

In a study of 10–14-year-olds in Canada, Mackey (2002) uses the metaphor of play to describe young people's involvement with traditional and
new media texts. This is a useful way of connecting writing, composing and
producing to engagements with different kinds of texts in which playing –
as in press play – as well as playing as active participation are evoked.
Mackey observes that:

> Playing makes room for the agency and energy of performers and
> calls for both internal and external accommodation to the activity: to
> play involves an engagement of the mind as well as appropriate
> behaviour of the body, a fruitful concept for considering the activities
> of text processing. Furthermore, the word *play* makes room for a kind
> of mental and dispositional 'on-switch' – an active commitment to the
> engagement – whose importance is sometimes overlooked in ordi-
> nary language about different kinds of text-processing.

(Mackey, 2002: 189)

Taking up this concept of playfulness and extending it beyond text processing to refer to an expanded communication repertoire is a central idea
in this book and one that is, of course, interwoven with our current
emphasis on improvisation and experimentation. Improvisation is at the
heart of such play, and always – as we suggest at the beginning of this
chapter – plays a part in the process of composition or production, even
if, in the case of heavily prescribed activities, that part is rather a small
one. We generate new possibilities *as we compose*, as we improvise and
experiment with what we know and what is possible. However, as the
examples in the previous section illustrate, improvisation also comes to
the fore when children are enabled to work across different media, and to

do so within open-ended opportunities for playful activity. In these contexts, we not only need to think about the process of composition as happening in relation to single texts, but *across* texts.

The ARG and 'Street' projects generated the kinds of motivating purposes and audiences that so many teachers work hard to provide when planning literacy provision. Importantly, though, the teachers did not plan precisely what the children would do. As with more established approaches to using drama and role-play in education (e.g. O'Neill, 1995), they allowed themselves to be led by the children and the narrative that emerged as children shared their responses to what happened; the texts children produced did not mark the end – or outcome – of an activity, but helped propel an overarching shared story forwards. This emerging story generated momentum and texts were created as needed or stimulated by events as they happened. In the 'Street' project, for example, the idea for the news report arose once an apparent crime had been detected. Colvert describes this kind of improvisational, collaborative story generation as 'ludic authorship', and argues that this kind of authorship is at the heart of many contemporary digital media practices. Her ARG project, she argues, provided the Year 6 designers 'with a playful context and purpose that shaped the way in which they engaged with their audience, and through a process of design the children developed their understanding of authorship as a communicative process' (Colvert, 2012: 124). Of course, this all means that the narrative itself is not 'owned' by a single author, something which is rather at odds with the way that curriculum and assessment frameworks construct children's literacy in school.

From a methodological point of view these teachers were also creative in their planning and teaching. Although they may not have made a radical departure from everyday practice, some of the important features of their work include the ways in which they:

- allowed children's ideas and interests to shape the direction of the narrative (e.g. the emergence of the 'birdsnatcher' as a character);
- allowed children to explore their ideas in a variety of media (e.g. pencil and paper, iPad apps and video);
- included a range of textual forms at different stages (e.g. drawings, maps, blogposts, poems and news features);
- encouraged both individual and collaborative engagement (e.g. poetry composition, blog comments and collaborative video production).

These orientations helped to provide the conditions for creative co-construction. Importantly, the teachers fundamentally respected the ways in which their children were actively making meaning and encouraged them to improvise and experiment with surprising results.

Planning for such possibilities, however, can be difficult to manage given other school demands, and this is something we return to in the final chapter of this book.

Summary

In this chapter we have explored the role of improvisation in composition, particularly in relation to digital media. We have considered some of the opportunities associated with promoting improvisation and experimentation and identified conditions and contexts in which improvisation might be encouraged. We have also considered some of the constraints and challenges that teachers may face and provided examples of ways in which teachers have overcome these.

....

QUESTIONS FOR REFLECTION

1. How do we make space for and foster improvisation?

2. How does improvisation fit with existing ways of thinking about the writing process?

3. What should we do as teachers when it feels as if things are getting out of hand?

....

7

USE PLAYFUL PEDAGOGIES

Schools have a role to play in providing risk-free environments in which children may follow passions, experiment, explore, gain feedback and consider alternatives. For teachers, this means adopting playful pedagogies and allowing work to take new or unexpected directions.

This chapter will:

- examine the use of a 'playful pedagogy' which involves a willingness to be open to unexpected directions as children make meanings using digital and non-digital resources

- provide examples of what can been achieved by encouraging children's playfulness

- explore how teachers can approach teaching playfully

- consider why a playful pedagogy may be particularly well-suited to developing 21st century literacies.

Improvisation and schooling

The sort of free-flowing explorations that are associated with the use of digital media in everyday life do not sit easily with ideas – official or otherwise – about what literacy might look like at school. Two student teachers from England, for example, reflect on why it can be difficult to integrate digital media within literacy provision:

> We gave them different websites to go to but because they had so many different topics it's quite hard and they ended up just looking at music websites and stuff and you'd constantly be checking every single person to check what they were doing cos you couldn't spend

your time with one person. You had to be constantly checking everyone else. 'Look – you can't go on that website – you have to be working.'

Within the whole school, creativity wasn't an issue, it wasn't embraced, it was just 'don't go there. We have to hit these targets, we have to hit these SATs, we have to tick these boxes' and several times, I heard the sentence, 'We can't waste an hour of children's education.' We have to prove we've done something in that hour that ticks a box that links to SATs.

(Cited in Burnett, 2011a)

These comments reflect some common concerns that teachers may face when trying to think and work with the digital in school. Giving children free rein could mean losing control, and this can feel very uncomfortable, particularly when teachers are under close scrutiny and held to account for what children achieve. In using classroom-based virtual worlds we have encountered similar issues – in one example, what was initially presented as an opportunity for unfettered exploration was seen by some teachers as difficult to contain and potentially chaotic (Merchant, 2009). Part of the *Active Worlds* environment called Barnsborough had to be 'sealed off', to prevent child-avatars from roaming too far. However, children quickly discovered that, by climbing on virtual objects, they could 'escape'. Eventually, members of the project team had to escort these unruly avatars back to safety! As amusing as this account of virtual truancy might be, it does show how the demands of time and task – and perceptions of the teacher's role – bear down on classroom life.

The pressure on teachers for their children to reach certain standards, which in many countries are measured by standardised tests, means that it can be difficult to give children the opportunity to explore for themselves. There is always the nagging worry that they might not be learning at all. The supposed certainty of things like progression in phonics and 'correct' ways to use exclamation marks are certainly more tangible than the processes (and sometimes even the products) of creative composition, particularly when the digital comes into play. As a result literacy can become 'fixed' in certain ways. Not just in terms of its breadth and reach, as explored in Chapter 2, but in ways that limit children's opportunity to improvise and take risks. And yet, ironically perhaps, it is the soft skills of collaboration and negotiation, as well as the capacity to improvise and experiment, that are valued in the world outside school. It is in recognition of this that many teachers have found creative ways of merging these apparently contradictory aims, and developed ways of working that incorporate improvisation and experimentation.

As the Year 6 class settle into their places for the afternoon, the teacher tells them he has something for them to watch. They turn to the electronic white-board now serving as a huge television screen. Strident music and rolling text signal the start of a news bulletin. As the first image hits the screen there is a gasp. It's the town they've been building in *Minecraft* over the last few weeks of Minecraft Club. Their town with its soaring towers, roller-coaster, monument and central hotel, all crafted by the children and woven into emerging stories and activities as they'd played with, in and around it. But disaster has struck. Before their eyes the buildings are disintegrat-ing, bits flying off and whirling through the sky (Figure 7.1). A tornado has hit their town and it wreaks havoc. A hushed silence descends on the classroom, and several children have tears in their eyes.

The iconic Bradborough statue

Figure 7.1   Tornado in action

This lesson was just one in a series in which Chris Bailey, the teacher, explored how to build on the children's enthusiasm for *Minecraft* – and for the weekly Minecraft Club they'd encouraged him to establish. In other lessons, he invited children to explore a desert island he'd created in *MinecraftEdu*, linked to work on the class novel – Michael Morpurgo's *Kensuke's Kingdom*. And one afternoon he introduced floating spheres to stimulate storymak-ing (as the appearance of the spheres prompted the children to ask what was going on). Of course, when Chris saw that some children were upset by the tornado he reassured them that they needn't worry. He had saved eve-rything they had created so they'd be able to return to it soon. In the mean-time, though, he had copied their world and released a 'tornado' mod into it, and it was this that had caused the destruction they'd just witnessed. He had used *Hackosaurus* to mix a screencast of the destruction with an exist-ing news report to create the news bulletin, and this worked as a powerful stimulus for further work linked to their topic on natural disasters.

In many ways what Chris did in producing the tornado report was very similar to what many primary teachers have been doing for years, using a thought-provoking or emotionally engaging stimulus to draw children into a narrative or imagined world in order to create 'authentic' experience related to ideas linked to a class topic or theme. Years ago teachers may have run off a few posters on a Banda machine and sellotaped them around school to stimulate children's discussion about a forthcoming (if fictitious) event. In this instance, easy access to the resources needed to capture and remix digital content meant that Chris was able to create something similar, but arguably more compelling. What is particularly interesting here though is the way that he took the cue from the children. The tornado would not have had its considerable impact if the children hadn't invested so much time, effort and imagination in creating their town in the first place. What Chris did was seize an opportunity to build on that investment and use it to open up new directions for the children to explore and of course, in doing so, generate lots of opportunities for them to create and communicate their own responses and ideas.

Chris was confident in experimenting with digital technologies, and so finding the *Minecraft* mods that effected the tornado, taking the screencast and remixing the news bulletin were not challenging for him. They were also things he enjoyed doing. Although these processes are much easier and quicker than they might seem to the uninitiated, other teachers may not be as confident or may just not be able to devote the time needed. This kind of activity, however, doesn't have to involve great technical expertise. As the use of *Kidblog* featured in Chapter 6 illustrates, easy-to-use and readily available applications and platforms can also be used to engage children in this way. What such activities do rely on, however, is a willingness to approach teaching playfully and to engage children in playful learning. Below we explore why *playfulness* might be important to children and teachers and why such approaches are not just facilitated by digital technologies, but are also highly appropriate when attempting to encourage children's creative and critical engagement with digital media.

Playfulness and learning

Play is rather an ambiguous term (Sutton-Smith, 1987) and 'play-based learning' can manifest in all kinds of ways. In the early years, the importance of play in learning has been extensively argued, and highly regarded models of early years provision – such as the Reggio Emilia approach in Italy and the Te Whāriki curriculum in New Zealand – have foregrounded the role of play in supporting wide-ranging aspects of children's learning, such as cognition, aesthetic awareness, critical thinking and language development (Broadhead, 2004; Moyles, 1989). Many early years practitioners bemoan the lack of opportunities for play as children enter more formal schooling, but there are practices that have a strong tradition throughout the primary years which build on very similar principles to play-based learning. These include drama and role-play, for example, and exploratory work (primarily in science and mathematics) where children engage in enquiry, collaboration and the kinds of 'possibility thinking' (Craft et al., 2012) that seem to be associated with creativity. Even if these activities differ from the kinds of things that some teachers might associate with play, we could certainly see them as *playful*. As the theatre educator Bernie DeKoven writes, '... playfulness, like humor, is a survival skill. It helps us adapt to change, to engage each other, to create community. Playfulness is flexibility, responsiveness, openness, sensitivity, awareness. It connects us to life' (DeKoven, 2015: 145). *Playfulness* can be thought of as an attitude or approach in which nothing is taken for granted and where established ways of doing things do not necessarily hold sway. The Playful Learning Centre, based in Helsinki, lists six conditions as part of their Manifesto for Playful Learning, producing a radical account of the power of play.

Manifesto for Playful Learning

- Question the authority of authority. Everything is up for grabs, teachers, knowledge values, epistemology – the works. What purpose does authority in learning serve? In whose interests? What's the point of the power relationships in education?
- Always draw attention to the fact that learning is all in the game, that it's a bodily, context-bound set of practices. It takes place in an immediate, often emotionally charged, social world. Don't ignore this fact. Don't pretend that it is otherwise. Challenge the myth that learning is only something that happens inside people's heads!
- Challenge the rules, the conventions of classroom interactions, the purposes of examinations and accreditation, the practices and processes of how learning is currently organized.
- Fight the boredom. Succeeding in education can often be a question of attrition. Keep finding ways to engage and motivate.
- Assert the agency of players. Too often children and young people are considered passive and empty. They are not. Learning is something people do, not something that is done to them.
- Consider the consequences or what's the point? Of education, of study, of learning? Winning and losing count: they matter. This is part of the game.

(Playful Learning Centre, 2015: 7)

Playfulness as defined in this way – with its emphasis on challenging rules and authority, giving children the lead and living for the moment – can sit rather uneasily with other classroom priorities and practices, particularly those governed by instrumental learning goals:

> Schooling is by definition not playful. It is focused on predictability – on performance, achievement, discipline, orderliness. Learning is something else. I think the very act of institutionalizing learning turns it, with few exceptions, into schooling. Giving grades, for God's sake, what a crazy thing. How do you grade someone's enjoyment, someone's delight in learning? Who is the real failure when a student doesn't learn?

> *(DeKoven, 2015: 147)*

It is hard to make space for playfulness if our eyes are on targets related to future success, and if as teachers we are held accountable for these targets, this may often be the case in relation to literacy provision. There is some irony here, however, given that it appears that a playful orientation towards classroom activities can encourage the very kind of experimentation and risk-taking that promotes language and literacy learning in the first place (Askeland & Maager, 2010; Cekaite, 2005; Waring, 2013). The light-hearted exchanges encouraged by a playful atmosphere, for example, provide a context in which children may try out new forms of language and see their effects; and being open to following the children's emerging interests can generate meaningful and motivating contexts for children to read and write a range of texts and to experiment with different modes of expression (e.g. Hobbs, 2013; Alper, 2013).

Although there is plenty to suggest that play can provide powerful learning experiences, the ongoing nature of many kinds of play, together with the sense that they may have no clear or predictable end-point, often makes it hard for educators to justify. However, when we look at adult engagement with new media, social networking, fanfiction and video-gaming, this same open-ended playful activity is often a key characteristic (Gee, 2003; Jenkins et al., 2006). Resulting from this open-endedness, there is a fluidity of meaning as individuals or groups take up ideas and themes, and improvise, develop or discard them as play unfolds. Studies of children's play often highlight this improvisational nature, which more often than not constellates around particular spaces and materials. For example, in a study of young children's play on and with piles of snow, Finnish researchers Rautio and Jokinen (2015) show how these different dimensions coalesce in both open-ended and game-like play events. Similar themes have also been taken up in studies of virtual play. For example, Marsh's (2010) account of young children's playful engagements with *Club Penguin* provides a rich exploration of this, whereas Beavis, Dezuanni and O'Mara (2017) illustrate how different dimensions of gameplay can be translated into primary and secondary classroom activity.

The importance of taking risks, trying out possibilities and challenging conventions are key themes in children's engagement with digital media. It is evident not only in online gameplay but also in the ways in which they create, consume and re-mix digital content, for example in *YouTube* videos, vlogs, fanfiction, etc. (see Chapter 8). And while many children may not actually create content as an independent activity, or post it online, they are likely to incorporate media references in their social play.

Playful teaching: going with the flow

Much guidance on effective teaching in recent years has focused on the need for teachers to set clear objectives that are shared explicitly with children and revisited at the end of lessons (Hattie, 2008). While such approaches may be useful in helping children and teachers clarify what is – and what has been – learned, if such approaches become routine, then free-flowing, playful approaches can be pushed out. In the tornado example that opened this chapter we can see how one alternative may be to improvise and work with learners' responses and in doing so open up new avenues for children to explore. Interestingly, after this lesson Chris reflected that perhaps his intervention had been too directive, and that maybe the children would have generated their own new directions if he had left them alone. There is no right response here, but his reflections highlight that playful teaching is a subtle art. It involves spending time listening to and watching what children are doing, saying and what they seem to be learning, in order to decide when to leave children to follow up their own interests, possibilities and questions, and when to step in (Burnett, Daniels & Sawka, 2016). At times this may involve engaging playfully alongside children, using humour and imagination and being prepared to work with the paradoxical (Gifford, 2004; Askeland & Maager, 2010). Rather than seeking to structure and frame, it involves improvisational and open-ended approaches. It may well be the case that much of this is learnt by the teacher through trial and error – perhaps teachers themselves need to take a few risks in developing a playful pedagogy.

Developing a playful pedagogy is particularly challenging in some contemporary contexts that are driven by strict sequences of skill acquisition and content knowledge that appear to require focused teacher guidance. The room for manoeuvre can be further constrained when mechanisms of teacher observation and accountability favour direct teaching and adherence to narrow curricular goals. Despite this, what we have observed in our work with schools, as documented in this book, is that creative teachers with a commitment to developing 21st century literacies can always find ways to innovate and to justify new approaches. Some approaches to introducing playful teaching in more structured contexts include:

- identifying specific times for introducing playful teaching (finding spaces within the weekly timetable or the year calendar);
- identifying a specific curriculum area or theme (developing an under-standing of character in literacy, or experience of particular writing genres);
- working with others on in-school or cross-school projects (often finding supportive partners, such as researchers, can help in this respect);
- developing a rationale for playful teaching (such as the development of creativity, learner autonomy, collaborative skills or 21st century literacies);
- considering appropriate ways of showing evidence of learning (online platforms can be particularly useful for this).

Evidence from research that has focused on a range of very different projects from school implementations of augmented reality games (ARGs) to those that have used and made videos in class seems to show that children's enthusiasm and teacher interest create a synergy which enriches and diversifies the kinds of learning that take place. This pro-vides a powerful reminder of the importance of playful teaching and can lead to a rather different assessment of the risks.

Virtual play

Issues about risk-taking and developing new professional strategies often emerge in work that documents the introduction of play with virtual worlds and videogames in the classroom (Merchant, 2009; Burnett & Merchant, 2016b; Bailey, Burnett & Merchant, 2017). Concerns about how much autonomy to allow children regularly come to the fore, and teachers often find that they have to rethink their role, in both the classroom and the virtual world. Over a number of years we have used the virtual world Barnsborough, built in the *ActiveWorlds* universe (see Figure 7.2), as a way of looking at the possibilities and challenges of *virtual play* in classrooms – we use the term virtual play to capture and describe the ways 'in which digital and networked media ... support play and play-related activities and interactions' (Merchant, 2016: 301).

The following extract from fieldnotes taken from in-world interactions with Year 5 pupils gives an impression of some of the unpredictability of this sort of virtual play and particularly the role ambiguity experienced by the adult researcher!

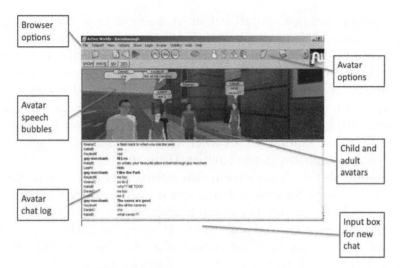

Figure 7.2   Screenshot of Barnsborough

Again as before excitement at seeing the tally of visitors. Some uncertainty about role – encouraging avatars to go in the 'right direction'. Should I? 15 avatars are in. They're dashing all over the place, falling in the sewage. Chaos as they get used to the navigation controls. I give occasional tips 'make your way to a ladder', 'over here', 'click on the door', etc. They don't seem curious about who I am (but maybe they are in the classroom). I'm also very interested that my view which is so partial just shows them flailing around and then eventually finding their way into the town square, it's almost as if their real voices are muted. I imagine that the classroom is quite noisy ... as they exchange tips or maybe express frustration. The speed at which I feel I have to act is interesting, too. I feel a bit like a guide. They begin asking me questions. I feel the need to show them places. It's a bit like being an adult helper on a school trip! Not quite sure what the teacher has in mind, but the activity of the kids keeps you busy. I have a technical frustration. I'm trying to gather screenshots as I go along, but because of the way I've configured my fly function, each time I do a screenshot I start to levitate. I find I can't stop, so I have to quit the world (disappear), then re-enter and teleport to where some of the kids (avatars) are. I wonder if they find this a bit perplexing. Some tell me to 'stop flying'. They think I'm showing off!

These are observations of children who are represented on-screen as avatars (see Figure 7.2) who have been invited to explore a 3D virtual world. They face no particular challenges and the environment is completely safe, and yet there are still some difficult questions for the adult. These are captured by comments like 'uncertainty about role', the possibility of guiding or 'encouraging' the children, feeling the 'need to show them places' and the idea of being an 'adult helper on a school trip'. Such comments are interwoven with descriptions of a rather chaotic atmosphere. In other accounts of children in this virtual world we have also documented the energetic atmosphere in classrooms as children provide commentaries on what they are doing in Barnsborough, call across the classroom to each other, or express frustration with technical issues (Burnett & Merchant, 2014, 2016b). While Barnsborough is no longer available, teachers may face similar issues when introducing other virtual worlds or open-ended sandbox games such as *Minecraft*.

But despite all this, it does seem that virtual play can be a particularly powerful experience for children, and can provide very rich opportunities for learning (Kafai, 2010). For example, Peppler (2013b) describes how a group of children worked in *Quest Atlantis*, a Multi-User Virtual Environment, to create buildings as part of an Architecture unit and share their experiences and creations using social media. Interestingly, in evaluations of virtual play in Barnsborough, teachers were more likely to express concerns about 'curriculum fit' and the investment of time than anxieties about the value of play or their own role in it (Merchant, 2013b). In other words we might conclude by suggesting that virtual play provides an important context in which children can set the agenda, and as platforms and applications become more sophisticated, more possibilities for integrating such work in the classroom are likely to arise.

Summary

This chapter suggests that playful pedagogies provide an important complement to the pedagogical strategies more usually associated with outcomes-led learning, and that such strategies may be particularly appropriate for supporting learning in an age of increased digital participation. We have noted that playful participation is a characteristic of everyday engagement with digital media and is therefore an important component of 21st century learning. Using digital media in this way already crosses over into the unofficial worlds of children's play. By building on children's interests and enthusiasms teachers can capitalise on this with their own playful interventions. Although there are some perceived risks in this kind of approach – particularly since play is unruly, unpredictable and sometimes subversive – the payoffs in terms of learner engagement and enjoyment are considerable. There are undoubted challenges in developing playful approaches and in many cases allowing children to set the agenda and to take the lead runs counter to prevailing discourses about teaching and learning. Nonetheless it is worth addressing these challenges, partly because of the links between playful experimentation and creativity but also because it forms a necessary part of exploring digital media.

QUESTIONS FOR REFLECTION

1. How might you collaborate with other classes or schools to generate playful opportunities?

2. How might you justify playful approaches to an inspector?

3. What tensions might there be between allowing children to follow interests and ensuring all are challenged and supported in developing their communication repertoires? How might you address these tensions?

8

CREATE OPPORTUNITIES TO WORK WITH THE PROVISIONALITY OF DIGITAL MEDIA

Although the school curriculum privileges the individual creation of fixed or final products, digital texts are often provisional, allowing them to be easily added to, reworked and remixed. Such practices have the potential to generate rich opportunities for children to reach new audiences, to give and receive feedback and to remix what others have done in ways that are both critical and creative.

This chapter will:

- explore the provisionality of digital media, i.e. the ease with which digital texts may be reworked

- investigate remix in popular media

- consider the potential for creativity and criticality generated through building opportunities for remix into literacy provision

- explore possibilities for reaching different audiences for what children produce

- describe ways in which feedback and response might be facilitated using digital media.

Stacey opens Word, then types football, underlines it, centres it, enlarges the heading, then goes to select **background**. There are no words spoken, but as Stacey opens the different **colour options** for the background, Michael says 'red and white, red and white' (the Sheffield United FC colours) until

(Continued)

(Continued)

Stacey selects two colours, red and white. Stacey then rapidly makes a series of alterations on the screen: she changes the size, font and location of the heading, centring it. Next they both sit back and put their hands on the back of their heads, elbows sticking out. Stacey asks, 'what shall we do?' Michael says, 'Here' and then types <u>foot</u>. Stacey comments, 'Take the thingy off' (referring to the **underline** function). Michael types: Football, football. Stacey reaches across and writes FOOTBALL, looks then deletes the word and rewrites it in lower case, presses return, notices that the grammar has been highlighted by the grammar check, investigates (looks at suggested revisions), ignores, changes font size, goes into **clipart** file, searches for football, scrolls down and chooses image, then moves to bottom right-hand corner, then searches, finds and inserts football player. Again, there is no talk during any of this. Stacey then deletes the 'football' title and replaces with 'what we like Y5/Y6'. Michael comments, 'We're year 6'. Stacey deletes Y5, then also deletes 'football, football, football'. (There is now no text on the page but the clipart remains.)

(From Burnett & Myers, 2006)

Observed during a classroom study of 8- and 9-year-old children's writing on screen, this is the kind of incident which many teachers still find extremely frustrating. Despite working together for several minutes, all this pair ends up with is an empty screen, nothing to work from, nothing to print, no evidence of either their decision-making or their design. And yet what we see in this vignette is a series of rapid decisions relating to layout, colour, font size and type, and woven into this, a confidence in the ease of changing, deleting, adding or otherwise revising. Moreover, much of what they produce is foraged from elsewhere – they go online to search for an image, use templates in *PowerPoint* to structure their design, and respond to the prompts about grammar and spelling provided by *Word*. This is a far cry from the painstaking process of altering texts with which many children are faced when working with pencil and paper (finding resources – searching the classroom to hunt down an eraser or sharpened crayons, for example, or rubbing out a word without leaving a mark or wearing a hole in the paper). While we may question whether what Stacey and Michael are producing is a carefully crafted text, we do see them able to work on their slides in a way that feels purposeful to them and with the skills and resources they need to act on the decisions they make as they go along. Moreover, what jumps out is the *provisionality* of digital texts. Texts can easily be reworked, remixed, taken from one source and copied, pasted and altered, and this means that new digital resources can be constructed out of existing material (Lessig, 2002).

Since the events described in this opening vignette, which occurred over a decade ago, the reworking of digital text has manifested in diverse forms. We are all familiar, for example, with the remixed news reports that proliferate online, through which creators have:

- laid down a new soundtrack;
- and/or edited together images or moving image footage from different sources;
- and/or overlayered words and images sourced from different sites.

At the time of writing, for example, a search for 'Trump remix video' generates 2,210,000 results that include multiple reworkings of snatches of the US president's media appearances: variously slowing down his speeches, setting them to music, overdubbing, ironically contrasting video footage or editing in excerpts from movies, cartoons, reports or TV programmes. Drag-and-drop digital editing programs such as *iMovie*, easily accessible via mobile devices, mean that it's possible for most people with the confidence, time, equipment and inclination to have a go at creating these kinds of playful and often 'critical' mashups.

Remix of course isn't new. Texts have always been reworked for different purposes and audiences. The disturbing fairy tales collected by the Brothers Grimm – such as Sleeping Beauty and Snow White – become something very different when 'Disneyfied', even texts such as the Bible get remade as different translations reflect the preoccupations of different eras, and sampling has long been a feature of rap. Some of the most creative and parodic remixes perhaps emerge from children's play. Seminal studies by the Opies (Opie & Opie, 1969) and more recently Willett et al. (2013) have documented how children play with and rework texts, whether these be playground rhymes, popular songs, TV programmes or *YouTube* videos, often in ways that are playful, anarchic or transgressive. Bailey's (2016) account of children's reworking of Band Aid's *Feed the World* as *Free the Sheep,* to protest against the trapping of some Minecraft sheep during an after-school Minecraft Club, is just one example of this kind of textual play. Such remix, we suggest, offers valuable opportunities for creativity, criticality and peer review.

Provisionality and creativity

Through drawing on established texts to generate new ones, remix blurs consumption and production (Merchant, 2013a) and, as such, it is a process that offers rich potential for creativity. One form in which remix is common and that has become increasingly popular in recent years is the short-form video, which we can find in a number of different arenas including *YouTube* instructional channels, television news features and music promotion. Its emergence is partly an effect of broader changes associated with the development of digital technology and the new forms of production and distribution that have arisen with it (Burn & Parker, 2003).

Many children see *YouTube* as a key source of entertainment, are avid consumers of such videos which are often linked to interests and hobbies (Ofcom, 2016) and see 'being a Youtuber' as a possible and viable career. Some Youtubers attract vast numbers of followers (as well as vast amounts of money): at the time of writing, for example, Smosh with their whacky comedy skits and parodies have 22,717,105 followers while vlogger Bethany Mota's video channel of recent purchases ('clothing hauls') and tips for personal grooming has 10,379,158. Many videos that are watched by young children seem to involve fairly mundane activities but link to their individual interests or hobbies, some of which can be very niche. 'How to' videos are particularly popular, linked, for example, to performing magic tricks, making things or doing make-up (Ofcom, 2016). Marsh (2016) analyses the increasing popularity of 'unboxing' videos, in which things – often technological devices such as laptops, mobiles or playstations – are described as they are unpacked from their boxes. Unboxing videos of toys – the unpacking of Kinder eggs for example – often gain large audiences of young children, perhaps because they deal with such familiar practices. Marsh describes one child's enthusiasm for an unboxing video on *EvanTube HD* (a channel produced in the US by Evan and his father with over 4 million subscribers at the time of writing) in which Evan unwraps a new Lego set and talks through the unpacking of all the parts and then building the model. Evan's status as a Youtuber, however, is unusual. While many children would like to make *YouTube* videos it seems that very few do so and those that do often run into problems and lose interest (Ofcom, 2016). Nevertheless such examples can provide inspiration for creative work using short-form video in the classroom.

Although the *YouTube* phenomenon has attracted the attention of scholars interested in youth studies and the emergence of a participatory culture (e.g. Burgess & Green, 2013), to date less attention has been given to its use in formal educational contexts. Higher education is an exception to this, with a growing number of reports on the use of short instructional videos on *YouTube* and other hosting sites (see Gilroy, 2010, for example). But there is still relatively little work on the educational possibilities of production, and particularly of examples of how that might be used to engage younger students. Notable exceptions are found in the work of Parry (2013) and Bulman (2017). Jeannie Bulman for example, worked with teachers as part of a cross-school storymaking project:

Children are documenting an imaginary space launch. This is their contribution to the development of a science fiction narrative shared between groups of children working in four different schools. After recruiting and training their crew this group decides to produce a short video that represents the initial stages of the journey. With the guidance of their teacher they combine existing free-to-use footage of a real launch with voice-overs and their own animation, showing lift-off and then mapping the intended trajectory though the Solar System using a model. This creative mashup is then shared with their partner schools as a way of developing the unfolding narrative.

In this project we can see primary school children involved in moving image production that is embedded within a larger project that provides both a purpose and a context for developing their skills in handling new media. Building on what they have seen elsewhere, these children are assembling media in a creative way, using techniques that are commonly employed in everyday contexts. This exemplifies principles set out in the previous chapters of this book, showing classroom activity that draws on and extends children's communication repertoires and harnesses their interest and enthusiasm. To reiterate, we use communication repertoire as an umbrella term for children's engagement with print and non-print media, digital and non-digital resources as well as on- and offline interaction. In the example above, found footage is combined with original material and stop-frame animation to produce a short-form video.

We see similar opportunities for production in Andrew Burn's description of the Making Machinima Project (Burn, 2016). During this project 11-year-olds made an animated film in the machinima style, an animation form emerging from computer games and virtual worlds. The students worked together to create a story about a computer games geek who ends up inside his own game and has to prevent an alien, Dr T, from taking over the world. Having done so, they made an animation using the 3D animation software tool, *Moviestorm*, designing sets, characters, music and so on, then animating the characters, adding dialogue, constructing shots and editing a final version. Making the animation involved coordinating a complex set of creative processes, all in the service of making a great film. It is worth noting, however, that these processes drew on skills and practices that are currently associated with a variety of curriculum subjects. This raises questions about how literacy itself gets remixed once we start working with digital media, and where – or even whether – we need to draw the boundaries around literacy activity in classrooms. As Burn argues:

This project demonstrates the importance of connecting children's understanding of processes of representation and their creative practices across the range of what school curricula constitute as distinct disciplines: in this case, literacy, media education, music, art and ICT [...]. Meanwhile, another kind of mash-up occurs: between the distinctive pedagogies of the arts, and the forms of social meaning-making they enable, along with the technologies they shape and are shaped by.

(Burn, 2016: 327-8)

Provisionality and criticality

As explored in Chapter 9, playful reworkings of familiar texts may be underpinned by a critical engagement which confronts stereotypical representations that children encounter in their everyday uses of digital media. In their everyday life online, children may well become very familiar with the ease with which information can be manipulated through everyday interactions with the internet. One child told, for example, how:

My cousin went on their website and got this bit on this snake and, cos he didn't want to be wrong, he copied it and changed it and printed it off and showed him that he was wrong ... he was changing the website ... cos he didn't want to look stupid.

(Cited in Burnett & Wilkinson, 2005)

Such experiences can give children insights into the decisions made by media producers in representing ideas, narratives and information, and can generate useful discussion about the different perspectives and priorities that underpin such decisions. Awareness of such considerations can be further enhanced as children engage as producers themselves, and sensitive work by teachers can support children when reflecting on how they and others position certain groups of people through what they produce.

We see this, for example, in Wohlwend's account of children's reworking of the Snow White story in one early years classroom during which they substituted the evil queen with Darth Vader, a move which led to extensive negotiations regarding how the Disneyfied version of the traditional tale could be merged with the *Star Wars* narrative. All the children were positioned by the teacher as directors who could decide together how the story should unfold. As they did so, they engaged in discussion about what the different characters might and could do. Wohlwend writes:

This engagement became a model for critical collaboration as this played text demonstrated the emergent nature of the storying process and the power of collaboration to challenge expected gender boundaries.

(Wohlwend, 2013: 22)

Provisionality and feedback

In some forms such as fanfiction, we see how authors draw on and rework original texts in the form of parody, satire or homage and post them online for others to read and review. Curwood, Lammers and Magnifico (2013) describe how adolescents create 'transformative works, which describe the kinds of writing and designing practices that take an original artifact and turn it into something with a new function or expression' (p. 677). Magnifico, for example, explores the writing that has sprung up around *Neopets*, the web-based game in which players look after virtual pets, writing for example for *The Neopian Times* and gaining feedback from other players. Curwood (2013) describes how one fanfiction writer, Cassie, wrote for *The Potter Games*, an online choose-your-own adventure game in which characters from Harry Potter are encountered in the world of the *Hunger Games*. Cassie was invited to contribute based on the strength of her existing *Hunger Games* based fanfiction. She approached the task by reading existing Harry Potter and *Hunger Games* novels, but then developed her story around one of the more minor Harry Potter characters. Drawing an audience from the extensive global fan bases for both Harry Potter and *The Hunger Games*, the game – and Cassie's contribution – attracted thousands of readers/players.

While perhaps a niche interest, fanfiction sites would seem to offer rich opportunities for authors to gain feedback on their writing from a wide readership that shares their enthusiasm for the story world with which they are working. The Harry Potter Fan Fiction site (https://harrypotterfanfiction.com) hosts over 80,000 stories and runs an awards ceremony to celebrate work voted for by site users. Readers' reviews provide authors with feedback from around the world. The story 'Accidentally on Purpose', for example, posted by Plum on 16 June 2017, is summarised as follows:

> Jenelle Clarke took Muggle Studies in a haze of love, riding the pink rush of a pheromone ridden wave, only to rudely find herself in the middle of a Scottish forest, with a map in her hands, banned from using magic and trapped with her *ex*-boyfriend and his new girlfriend.
>
> She was willing to risk *everything* to get out.

The reader is informed that the story, 'Contains profanity, Mild violence, Scenes of a sexual nature, Substance abuse, Sensitive topic/issue/theme.' By 2 August, the story had already received seven reviews by enthusiastic readers. One, The Tenth Weasley, commented:

> *2nd August 2017:*
>
> AH ugh the tension you created in this chapter was just so perfect. I could feel disaster coming from the very first line – nothing good could

come from Jenny and Flora being extremely drunk and friendly. I feel so bad for her: James cheated on her, ignores her in favour of Jenny, is a generally s*itty person ... and when she said 'I would never ... No', ugh :(It's a shame that she's getting caught up in the story of James and Jenelle, and she's not even fully involved, just stuck on the periphery. I'm glad Jenny actually stood up for her, even while she was blaming James for the situation at the same time ... another example of the reality you bring to these characters; they're not plainly written teenagers with a black and white sense of morality.

I only saw this coming because of TWY but nevertheless it was still exciting to read. The whole last scene was sooo frustrating because even while they're finally being forthcoming they're still communicating terribly. "You're a f*cking moron," I hissed back.' So funny, so typical of Jenny to do – seeing a chance to insult James even if it isn't the wittiest. The whole argument in general was well written. I feel like if I was reading this for the first time, without any prior knowledge of TWY, it'd be as if I was there as a fly on the wall, watching it unfold in real time, on the edge of my proverbial seat (which I still kind of was anyway), shocked at what you were revealing.

Dom is irritating me – she's so invasive and problematic. I love her as a character and I know she isn't a bad person really, but I don't think I could deal with being friends with her. You can sense that she knows she's messed up and is scrambling to do something about it, I'm unsure if this something is to fix the situation or to cover her own skin so James and Jenny don't hate her.

If I was going to say anything not entirely positive, it would be that this chapter is maybe a little too full? There's a lot going on here, what with Flora and Jenny's first proper interaction, the fallout of Jenny and Oliver, Jenny kissing Luke, Jenny shouting at Dom, Jamelle argument number one, Jenny telling Flora about James, Jamelle argument number two. I suppose that this is reminiscent of how a night drinking as a teenager would go – so much stuff happens and there's not much time to deal with it. But still, it felt a tiny tiny bit rushed. Omg pls don't hate me.

Another suggestion; have you ever listened to Julia Michaels? Her new stuff is good for inspiration – for me anyway – and I thought about her song 'Worst in Me' while reading this.

Anyway, v good exhilarating and dramatic chapter, I can't wait to see what happens next, especially because I feel like this is nearly all new material! xoxo

To which the author replied ...

Author's Response: Urgh yeah Flora so does not deserve any of what's happening to her. James and Jenelle are so volatile with each other when they're not together, all they do is cause destruction to so many people. I feel terrible for Flora too!! But she's going to prove to be resilient and a lot stronger than any of them realise. I mean I think it's still crazy that they still manage to be realistic in such heightened and crazy situations LOL but it's what I'm trying to achieve so THANK YOU!!

Hahaha yes, that question was more for non-TWY readers but I'm so happy it was still tense and exciting! And omg YES, that's exactly what I wanted it to come across as – a frustrating clash that feels like it's going nowhere. Like they're both FINALLY talking to each other but they just cannot get past the points they want to make so it's like they might as well not be communicating at all.

Dom is someone I just constantly feel bad about writing. Like (and I hope this doesn't give stuff away, though I'm not sure how it would lol) it's almost how I imagine Rowling would feel, in a way, writing Peter Pettigrew as he turned traitor. You just feel bad about making someone you want to be good be the person they honestly are. Dom IS loveable and does have redeeming qualities, but if what James says she's done is true – and Jenny can't think of why James would lie about that even if she has no idea why Dom WOULD do something like that – then she's set herself on a path that's going to be hard to come back from.

OMG, please don't think I'd ever hate you?!! One of the purposes of reviews is to receive constructive criticism so i genuinely LOVE to read this. And the thing is I agree with you completely! This chapter is absolutely CHOCKED with significant things that are almost written in a very insignificant way. Kind of tossed in there with the expectation that we'd have more time to mull on things but I can say the rush WAS intentional and somewhat needed. All of this was intended to finally PUSH Jenny into action and stop sulking about. I mean I wish I could've written this in the course of several chapters but the story needs to plunge on. And while we do finally slow the pace down again, it's still going to rush forward lol.

Okay ... I just listened to that song and I'm freaking CONVINCED I wrote it about Jamelle and gave it to her to sing lmao. It's impossible and not true but I'm ... shook. It's been added to my playlist, done and

DONE. Loved it. I EFFING love song suggestions. idk why but when people say this fic/the characters remind them of a song I lose my mind LOL.

Truly!!! The next few chapters are COMPLETELY new and while they have a few familiar bits, I can confirm like 98% of it is new stuff.

LOVED THIS REVIEW AS ALWAYS. And as always my responses are too much and I'll be shocked if u manage to get through this wall of text lol. But I just love your reviews!! Thank you!!! Can't wait for you read the next chapter. P xx

Through the review process, we see Plum and her avid readers engage together with unfolding events. Reviewers, like authors, care what their audience (the author) thinks, and may devote considerable time and effort to writing reviews, foregrounding their response to the story. In this case, the reviewer offers plenty of feedback on parts they liked as well as some very gently phrased critique. We can see how The Tenth Weasley is keen not to offend Plum, and how Plum in turn tells The Tenth Weasley how important the review is for the development of the work. This combination of response, critique, support and care helps sustain an ongoing author/reviewer relationship and could well provide a useful framework for feedback in schools. The Harry Potter Fan Fiction site is primarily for teens and adults, and trying to develop the kind of autonomous community of writers/reviewers that frequent fanfiction sites would be difficult in school contexts (Lammers et al., 2017). However, the opportunity to reach an enthusiastic readership and gain feedback on writing would seem to offer great potential for young readers and writers, and many teachers have explored ways of encouraging similar opportunities for authorship at school, encouraging learners to post their creations and gain feedback from each other, using online platforms such as *Edmodo*. Perhaps unsurprisingly the extent to which such feedback is formative varies; it tends to be congratulatory rather than critical (Magnifico et al., 2015). However these kinds of opportunities can engage peers in reading each other's work, and as such can offer a valuable chance for children to feel part of a community of writers and to reach an audience for their writing. Chapter 4, for example, describes how children in two schools used blogs to share thoughts about an emerging shared narrative (in the form of images, writing, video and so on). Children were encouraged to comment on these, such comments sometimes being focused on content and sometimes on form.

Of course, even when comments from readers aren't forthcoming or those that are offered appear rather superficial, the sense of audience can still help shape what children write. In 'The Street' project (Chapter 6), the Year 3 teacher (Adam Daley) noted that the writing the children posted online differed from the writing they usually did – both quality and content seemed to shift in response to the real audience of Year 5 children at another school (Monkhouse et al., 2017). In another collaborative project, 8–9-year-olds from a rural primary paired up with 9–10-year-olds from a primary school in an urban setting. The collaboration began with the exchange of 'virtual shoeboxes' – photographs of a collection of artefacts that each child collected to represent their interests. Having received their partner's shoebox, children emailed their partners to probe each other's interests further (Dickinson et al., 2006). Children told us that they were very conscious of what their unfamiliar partners might think of what they had written. One commented:

> I just want to do it right – cos I think the school's quite posh. Yes – I don't like people who think I'm a little town boy – I am one but I don't want them to think that.
>
> *(Cited in Burnett & Myers, 2006)*

Collaborative projects such as these not only generate opportunities for feedback, but the sense of a 'real' readership that can sharpen children's sense of what and how they want to communicate.

In the two projects above the 'audience' was planned and communication happened in the bounded online space of a password-protected message board. In other projects, audiences for children's work have been reached more serendipitously. Martin Waller (2013), for example, describes how he developed the use of *Twitter* with his Year 2 class of 6–7-year-olds. While only followers 'approved' by Martin could access their tweets, the use of *Twitter* provided valuable opportunities for children to share and reflect on their learning. Responses from followers often promoted further activity, for example as they asked them to tweet photos of their work. Dan Power and Wil Baker (Monkhouse et al., 2017) also used *Twitter* to contact Brian Moses, the poet who had compiled the poetry anthology they were reading in class. As a result of the exchange Brian Moses generously stepped in to judge the class haiku competition and provide insightful feedback on the winning poem. Planning for children to write for real audiences and purposes is certainly nothing new in literacy education, but opportunities to share using digital platforms amplify the possibilities available for reaching new audiences and for gaining rapid feedback on what children have written or produced.

Remix: what's allowed?

Thinking about remix raises questions about copyright and intellectual property. As remix has become an ever more common dimension of everyday life, ideas about sole authorship have started to feel very shaky and legal and ethical frameworks perhaps need revisiting. How far should established approaches to copyright be maintained at a time when boundaries between consumers and producers are increasingly blurred? How far should we be able to take what others have made and remake it for our own purposes? These questions have been the subject of much debate for some time (e.g. Lessig, 2002, 2003). However, it is important to be aware of the current legal position regarding copyright, recognising that the legal position may differ from country to country. Work given a Creative Commons licence may (depending on the precise licence) be freely used, distributed and remixed as long as authors or producers are acknowledged. Beyond this, works should not be reproduced unless permission has been granted, and while the proliferation of remixed material on the web would suggest otherwise, some organisations, such as film companies and music labels, are very active in demanding that any copyrighted material is taken down or paid for. There are exceptions, however, where copyrighted materials are used for non-profit-making purposes, and where the use of them is unlikely to interfere with sales of the original. In the UK, for example, some notable exceptions include:

- use of limited material for purpose of 'parody, caricature or pastiche', e.g. a small fragment of a film or soundtrack might be used;
- educational use (as long as this is not done for commercial purposes, and as long as there is no licensing scheme in place).

(Intellectual Property Office, 2014)

These exceptions relate to the notion of 'fair dealing' which is the legal term used to decide whether use of copyright material infringes copyright. The UK Intellectual Property Office (2014) expands on the notion of fair dealing as follows:

There is no statutory definition of fair dealing – it will always be a matter of fact, degree and impression in each case. The question to be asked is: how would a fair-minded and honest person have dealt with the work?

Factors that have been identified by the courts as relevant in determining whether a particular dealing with a work is fair include:

- does using the work affect the market for the original work? If a use of a work acts as a substitute for it, causing the owner to lose revenue, then it is not likely to be fair
- is the amount of the work taken reasonable and appropriate? Was it necessary to use the amount that was taken? Usually only part of a work may be used

The relative importance of any one factor will vary according to the case in hand and the type of dealing in question.

(Intellectual Property Office, 2014: n.p.)

In any case, it is certainly worth double checking current regulations before you post or share anything children have created to a general audience.

Summary

In this chapter we have explored the pedagogical opportunities associated with the provisionality of digital media. We have described the ease with which digital texts can be produced, reworked and distributed and some of the ways in which this plays out in life beyond educational settings. We have considered how such practices have the potential to generate rich opportunities for children to reach new audiences, to give each other feedback, and to remix what others have done in ways that can be both critical and creative. We have provided some examples to illustrate some of the ways in which educators have sought to capitalise on these opportunities in the classroom.

QUESTIONS FOR REFLECTION

1. Think of examples of provisionality from your own experience of working with digital media. In what ways has this been helpful or unhelpful?

2. In what sorts of ways might parody videos and remixes be considered to be 'critical' and how might such practices be adapted for the classroom?

3. What opportunities could be provided for peer feedback in classrooms, and how might this draw on some of the practices described in this chapter?

9

PROVIDE CONTEXTS THAT FACILITATE CRITICALITY

Advocates of critical literacies argue that literacy education must address the power relationships perpetuated through and around texts through critical engagement. Calls for greater criticality have intensified in recent years and are linked to fears about internet safety, commercialism, the stereotypical depictions associated with games and virtual worlds, and the need for discerning use of online resources. Demonising the texts young people use in everyday life is likely to achieve little. Providing contexts in which young people may critically consider the practices in which they engage, and how they position themselves and are positioned by others with opportunities to rework texts to reflect alternative experiences, is important.

This chapter will:

- consider why it is important to facilitate a critical dimension to children's media production

- explore how children may position themselves or may be positioned by the online communities in which they participate

- propose a 'critical networks model' through which children may be supported to consider critically the digital media they encounter and the practices in which they engage

- consider how children may be encouraged to use digital media safely and advantageously.

I really like *scratch*, I've used the Program for many years. I was last year shown to the home site. It was a great place, I found many cool projects, people, and ideas. Through *scratch*, I have achieved great personal growth.

(Continued)

(Continued)

But that was last year ... even last year this was kind of evident, but the problem has grown. Its every where I go now, there Isn't a single time I log onto *scratch* and dont run into one of these problems ... There are Haters on this site ... lots of 'em. They go around down grading any one they dont like. I even got a hate message, and it was the first message I got on my first project. There is also lots of bad words on this site. *Scratch* is primarily a site filled with little kids. But there are a bunch of famous, or semi-famous scratchers out there that are older, and they use bad words. some of them over use bad words. Being that you have your eye on the site (I hope) I'm pretty sure you know who they are. [...] I know that you cannot change the people that use your server, but there must be something you can do to try to change all this disgusting behavior ... right?

(Cited in Brennan, 2016)

The comments above are taken from an email sent by a young *Scratch* user to administrators of the online community of *Scratch* creators hosted by MIT (scratch.mit.edu), where users can share what they produce and give and receive feedback. It was collected by Karen Brennan for her study of young users' sense of audience when participating in an online community.

As we explore in other chapters, a distinctive feature of life in the 21st century is the use of digital media to join with others to pursue shared interests, to collaborate or simply to have fun through writing fanfiction, social media, virtual play or multiplayer gaming, for example, as well as through participating in citizen science, political activism, consumer review sites and support groups. Jenkins et al. (2006) referred to this phenomenon as the emergence of a participatory culture, in which members 'believe their contributions matter, and feel some degree of social connection with one another' (Jenkins et al., 2006: 3). The notion of a participatory culture chimes well with ideas about communities of practice that have been popular for some time with many educators (see Lave & Wenger, 1991). They offer the promise of mutual support, peer feedback and collaboration providing rich possibilities for learning. Gee's work on the affinity spaces that grow up around videogaming communities (Gee, 2003) and the varied and diverse 'constellation of literacy practices' observed by Steinkuehler (2007) provide vivid examples of how this sort of peer learning can take place.

However, access to and participation in such practices is decidedly uneven, and brings with it concerns about safety, trustworthiness and unwelcome attention. At the time of writing, the notion of fake news – in all its manifestations – is taking flight, destabilising trust in the flow of information; moral panics regarding online safety, privacy and identity theft persist; concerns about links between social media and terrorism abound; and questions are raised about how we can ever gain purchase on alternate viewpoints when so much of what we read – from friends on social networking sites to targeted advertising – may simply reinforce our existing viewpoints and interests. And then there are debates about the data collected on us as we surf the net and the purposes – commercial, political or otherwise – to which those data are or could be put (Fuchs, 2017). Given that so much of life is played out online, however, the need to facilitate *critical* literacy practices that confront these kinds of issues has arguably never been more pressing.

In thinking about how we might promote critical literacy practices in primary schools, it is worth recognising that 'critical literacy' can be understood in different ways. In what follows we distinguish between what might be called 'small c' and 'Big C' critical literacy. We see 'small c' critical literacy as being focused on supporting children to be discerning users, while 'Big C' critical literacy starts from the assumption that everyday life is framed by unequal power relations, upheld in part by the language and texts we use. While recognising that these two concepts are intimately related to one another, we explore them separately in order to tease out different emphases which we see as central to developing 21st century literacies.

'Small c' critical literacy

The following transcript, taken from an interview conducted over a decade ago with a group of 10–11-year-olds, illustrates some aspects of 'small c' critical literacy. The rather disingenuous interviewer (Cathy) had asked the group to tell her how to find information using the internet:

Ella:	So if you don't know the website you put in, so say you want some certain TV programme or something and say you just type in the name of that programme and it
Katy:	with Simpsons, you might want to go onto BBC first
Ella:	yeah
Katy:	cos they put the Simpsons on
Ella:	so if you put in BBC and then it comes up with a little BBC search engine and you put in The Simpsons on there, it comes up with proper The Simpsons.
Katy:	The official website
Interviewer:	If I went through Google, I'd get a list would I?
Josh:	Yes – it's searching for websites that have Simpsons in the title.
Michael:	It doesn't really work cos once I was searching for The Simpsons and I found something about mortgage payments.

Zac:	Yeah it'll be like the name of a company. On Google it says something like this search took 0.2 seconds and we found 300,000 results.
Katy:	It's normally more than that. It's like 20,000 million.
Michael:	So just look at the 1st page.
Interviewer:	Why?
Josh:	Cos otherwise the others are just rubbish ... they're nothing to do with it.
Ella:	Usually the first page is the most appropriate thing.
Katy:	The Internet doesn't really know.
Ella:	It's just stabbing in the dark.

(Cited in Burnett & Wilkinson, 2005)

This interview reveals not just the confidence with which these children approached the internet and what they had learned through use, but some of the challenges and pitfalls associated with locating information: judging reliability, for example, and navigating the vast number of sources available. The children's comments suggest that they approached such challenges in similar ways to many adults (just looking at the first page of search results for example), and that there is a place for exploring strategies that may be more effective or productive. These are the kinds of skills and orientations that might be addressed through 'small c' critical literacy, e.g. being able to:

- design and conduct internet searches judiciously, e.g. deciding which search engines and search terms and so on to use;
- weigh up whether or not a search has been successful;
- make judgements about the origin – and likely reliability – of specific sources;
- use strategies to help evaluate the reliability of information generated through searches, e.g. through triangulating sources;
- identify bias, examining images and moving images, etc. as well as words.

'Small c' critical literacy is captured in various ways in current curricula and curriculum guidelines, appearing in aspects of 'information literacy', 'critical thinking' and 'digital literacy', for example. However it is packaged, though, it is an increasingly common focus for national curricula. The National Curriculum in England, for example, states that children in locally maintained schools should:

> use technology safely and respectfully, keeping personal information private; identify where to go for help and support when they have concerns about content or contact on the internet or other online technologies.

(DfE, 2013)

Reflecting a growing consensus that such skills are an integral part of every-day life, the Organisation for Economic Cooperation and Development (OECD) has recently called for a focus on the critical reading of web-based material in schools and information literacy is integrated within the international Programme for International Student Assessment (PISA) tests (OECD, 2011). As explored in Chapter 4, many children will bring such skills with them to school, based on their informal experiences of working and playing online, although of course this cannot be taken for granted (Livingstone & Haddon, 2009). In building on children's diverse experiences in schools, the most effective opportunities are likely to derive from using the internet for reasons that matter rather than from contrived exercises. Hobbs (2013), for example, reports how a chance encounter with a homeless person while on a class trip with a class of 9-year-olds in Philadelphia, USA prompted an investigation into homelessness. Children searched the web, weighing up sources and critically analysing media representations. Extending this research they interviewed community members and advocates for the homeless. Children presented what they discovered in the form of a digital comic which was then distributed to peers, parents, teachers and the wider school community.

Discernment in internet use is clearly a vitally important part of 21st century literacy provision. However, if we are to realise opportunities for children to be more active participants in the world around them, then they need to learn more than discernment. While the idea of the internet as a democratising force enabling participation for all is certainly attractive, we know that the reality is quite different. Like other aspects of our lives, internet use is characterised by inequity and the workings of power. This is where what we are calling 'Big C' critical literacy comes in.

'Big C' critical literacy

We use 'Big C' critical literacy to refer to approaches influenced by the critical pedagogies developed by influential thinkers such as Freire and Apple (Apple, 1982; Freire, 1985; Freire & Macedo, 1987). If, as these seminal thinkers argued, power circulates in this way, then language and text become key sites for understanding how different groups are positioned, both locally and in the wider world. Kellner and Share (2007: 65), for example, suggest that critical media pedagogy should approach media as a process of social construction and emphasise:

- relationships between representation, ideology and power;
- production, e.g. making films or websites that address under- or misrepresented themes;
- analysis and use of different tools and codes for representation (e.g. linked to information literacy, multimodality);
- the role of audience in actively making meanings.

Silvers, Shorey and Crafton (2010) provide a good example of this sort of stance in documenting the work of a class of 6- and 7-year-olds in Chicago that took place at the time of the Hurricane Katrina disaster in New Orleans. The children, who referred to themselves as the Hurricane Group, came to an understanding of larger issues of poverty and racism through the sensitive support of their teacher who drew on the extensive media coverage and multiple resources including the 'internet, pictures, news stories, books, personal stories, magazines, videos' (p. 389) to develop a critical understanding of the impact of the disaster and how it was portrayed. Group discussions based on these resources were guided by key questions:

- Whose voices are heard? Whose voices are absent?
- What does the author/illustrator want the reader to think/understand?
- What is an alternative to the author/illustrator's message?
- How will a critical reading of this text help me change my views or actions in relation to other people?

(Silvers, Shorey & Crafton, 2010: 388)

Here the teacher, working from a social justice perspective, built on the children's interest and introduced criticality across a range of media.

Others have focused on critical examination of the popular media which are so integral to many children's lives outside school, exploring how films, games, social networking sites, etc. work to construct gender, race, ethnicity, sexuality and disability in ways that reflect and help sustain inequities. However, such work can be problematic. While stereotypical depictions may well be prevalent in many popular forms, critical interrogation of children's favourite characters and narratives may simply spoil children's enthusiasm for them and risk reinforcing ideas that such texts are somehow less worthy than those sanctioned by school (Buckingham, 2003; Parry, 2013). Moreover, if critique works in opposition to children's cultures, then such approaches may well be disempowering rather than empowering.

Rather than focusing on explicit critique of popular media it may be more valuable to plan open-ended opportunities for children to play through the narratives associated with popular media. Such opportunities may well generate the kind of critical engagement that educators might wish for, but in ways that are led by the children themselves. If you have ever listened to children playing with the lyrics of a popular song, you will know how the words are frequently remixed, often counter to the meanings intended in the original. Dyson's work illustrates how children rework popular narratives and characters through their play (e.g. 1993, 2003). Of course there may be times when teachers encourage children to reflect on such play, but in doing so they will work from and with children's understandings and intentions. Rather than focusing critical literacy on 'texts' as if they are finished artefacts, this approach focuses on the meanings that are negotiated *between* readers/viewers and texts, and allows children the space to work with these meanings rather than attempting to stand back from them.

Kendrick, Early and Chemjor (2017) meanwhile explore how young girls at a Kenyan girls' journalism club took up opportunities to use video in ways that ultimately enabled them to intervene in local politics. Interestingly, the video cameras were introduced in an open-ended and unstructured manner and the girls took up the cameras in ways that served their immediate interests and concerns. Early examples included playfully recording their friends and teacher, but later the girls turned to the cameras when they returned from a school holiday to find that a portion of school land had been claimed by a local resident, and drew on their film to protest the case and also conducted interviews with leading officials. It is possible that the lack of structure in the early stages and the opportunity to explore and experiment with the cameras as a means of framing their lives – to take control of them in ways that meant something to them in the moment – prepared the way for their later seizing the opportunity to use the cameras to support their activism. As Kendrick et al. (2013: 416) write,

> they were able to try on the language of others, to 'taste' the profession of journalist (Bakhtin, 1935/1981) in a lower-risk, more playful context before entering a more high-stakes professional community, with all its inherent risks and responsibilities.

Becoming critical

'Big C' critical literacy focuses not just on the trustworthiness of information, but on whose interests it serves and ultimately how we might intervene in what's going on around us to make it more equitable (for ourselves or others). Importantly, approaches to critical pedagogy tend to go beyond identifying the workings of power to empowering learners to take control of their own lives and act on the world around them. Giroux (1994: 90), for example, argues for a need to find 'spaces' where meanings can be 're-written, produced and constructed rather than merely asserted' (Giroux: 1994: 90). In a similar vein, Janks' (2010) model of critical literacy combines four dimensions: *domination* (a focus on language and power); enabling *access* to dominant discourses; the acknowledgement and facilitation of a *diversity* of discourses in classrooms through which dominant discourses may be interrogated; and *design* through which learners are supported in developing their own, often subversive or alternative, meanings. In each of these we can see how 'small c' and 'Big C' critical literacies intersect: skills and orientations associated with design and discernment are put to use for reasons of empowerment.

This kind of criticality underpins various online practices that work to parody aspects of social, cultural and political life, such as the Trump remixes described in Chapter 8. Indeed media educators have argued for many years that one of the most effective ways to understand the processes of text making (and what influences decisions made during these processes) is to engage in media production. In the digital age, media production may also generate powerful opportunities for children to act on (not just in) the world around them. As Luke (2012) argues, 'Reading and writing are always about something in the phenomenological world and they can be used to construct, build, imagine and critique other possible worlds – as a passport to other spaces, journeys and places' (p. 12). Comber and Nixon (2013), for example, describe how critical pedagogies were combined with place-based pedagogies during a project with immigrant children in a primary school in Adelaide, South Australia. Children used a range of media to explore their memories and experiences of the local area and in doing so established themselves as valued members of the community.

A critical literacy framework for the 21st century

Critical literacy frameworks have provided an important counterpoint to skills-based models of literacy provision, foregrounding social equity rather than market efficiency. However, the growth in distributed, participatory practices raises other questions about the kind of critical literacy needed for the 21st century. To begin with, distinctions between production and consumption are increasingly blurred, and isolating texts to examine and work with is ever more problematic. A screenshot may frame a webpage in time, but its very textuality depends on the regular updates and hyperlinks lost through that freezing, and of course the exponential growth of mobile technologies has intensified opportunities for literacies to interweave with everyday practices, tasks and activities. Moreover, given the social and participatory practices in which many children are involved, children, more than ever, do not just need to evaluate texts but to consider who they are communicating with. We need a critical literacy that can work with the *fluid and distributed* nature of contemporary literacy practices.

E-safety – perhaps understandably – is the issue that has gained most traction in discussions about children and the internet, networks and unknown and/or anonymous others (this is discussed in Chapter 2). However, there are other ways in which the internet brings us into relationship with the world around us. What we do online is closely bound up with economics, politics and environmental concerns. Of course this isn't new. Complex relations of economics, politics and environmental consequences are folded into most of what we do and always have been – in the products we use and activities in which we engage. But what perhaps is new is the role of digital media in enabling those relations, and the active part that most people play – through what they do online – in *upholding* those relations (Facer, 2011). As Facer writes:

> Working with these technologies does not merely mean 'using' networks that act as a platform or a neutral stage for our advanced human intelligence. Instead we are working and integrated with networks that are employing different ways from us of solving problems and 'thinking' about things. The global collective intelligence we are developing, then, is not just human, it is also machine.
>
> *(Facer, 2011: 67)*

This complex context generates many questions for us as educators and also as individuals and members of different communities and groupings: what kind of legacy is left by our digital footprint, for example? Who owns the websites we use and who manages the algorithms? And how far are these managed by people and how far are these mechanisms delegated to artificial intelligence? Importantly, what we do online everyday has implications not just for our own lives, but the lives of others. There is not only a safety dimension then but an ethical dimension. So, the implications for literacy education proliferate. We need not just consider how to ensure children use the internet safely and in ways that are discerning, but how individuals can position themselves through their participation in such networks, and how far this is ethical and advantageous to them and others (or not). The meshing of digital media in everyday life raises critical questions about how we relate to one another and the world around us. Asking 'how are we positioned by texts?' and 'whose interests does this serve?' suddenly becomes rather complicated. As well as developing critical literacies that focus on the examination and analysis of language and text, we need to focus on what people do *through* texts.

Exploring the relationship between practices, networks and identities

In thinking about how we might frame critical literacy for the 21st century, we suggest a 'critical networks model' (Burnett & Merchant, 2011) that draws attention to three interrelated dimensions:

- **Practices**: what we do with digital media, in or around digital environments.
- **Identities**: how we position ourselves and are positioned by others through our digital media practices.

- **Networks**: the social and textual networks in which we participate and in which we are enabled to participate (knowingly, willingly or otherwise) through our uses of digital media.

Rather than focusing primarily on text, this model shifts the focus to what people do, and to how this relates to broader social and textual networks (see Figure 9.1). It provides a way of thinking about how far people's practices enable (or disable) their participation in different networks, on how they are positioned through these practices and networks, and consequently how far such participation is empowering (or not).

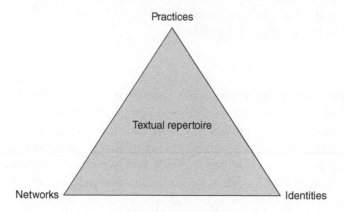

Figure 9.1 Critical networks model – critical literacy in the 21st century

(Burnett & Merchant, 2011)

Developed specifically to account for critical literacy in relation to social media we suggest that the critical networks model is a helpful starting point for thinking about digital media practices more broadly. Even so Clare Dowdall's study of three pre-teenage girls' use of the social networking site, *Bebo*, in 2010–11 provides a useful illustrative example. Dowdall (2017) explores the different ways in which individuals used *Bebo* and drew on the possibilities it offered:

- Jenii used comments and posts to position herself in relation to others, signalling shared interests in popular culture for example, and spent time organising and editing her profile page. Dowdall describes how she 'invested in it and enjoyed crafting her profile to create a pleasing textual artefact. She described her profile with pride as My *Bebo*, and one of the main quests was to seek admiration and kudos through the look of her page' (Dowdall, 2017: 173).
- Chloe was keen to present herself as someone who wasn't 'addicted to' or 'controlled by' *Bebo*; she checked others' pages for negative postings and played a hacking game with her friends through which they shared

passwords and playfully changed each other's profiles. Her use of *Bebo* seemed very much designed to maintain her immediate circle of friends – her 'crewage' – rather than interact with wider networks. Dowdall describes Chloe as a 'discerning and critical user of *Bebo*, using it carefully to exert control over her social world while enacting her friendships' (Dowdall, 2017: 174).

- Elley also spent time viewing others' profiles and curating her own but was cautious about what she presented, aware of how her profile might be taken or interpreted by others. This awareness seemed to inhibit what she did rather than empower her to take control. She was, in Dowdall's words, 'a critical agent, but inhibited rather than empowered as an origi- nator of text through her critical awareness' (Dowdall, 2017: 174).

Dowdall's analysis echoes many of the themes introduced above. It high- lights for example how these individuals worked to manage how they presented themselves to others, working to craft *identities* through care- fully designing text and image through repeated posts. Potter describes this process as an act of curation involving 'the collection, production and exhibition of markers of identity through time in both digital pro- duction and social media' (Potter & Gilje, 2015: 123). What they did though – their *practices* – varied, and they seemed differently inclined to play with what was on offer: while Chloe introduced the hacking game, Jenii experimented with design. They reinforced *networks* through their *Bebo* use – mainly existing circles of friends – and were cautious about how they may be positioning themselves within other networks too: Elley was more reserved in her postings, while Chloe worked actively to guard against unwelcome engagement from others. While this brief summary cannot do justice to Dowdall's analysis, it does provide an example of how different practices, identities and networks can intersect in ways that are variously empowering or disempowering for individuals.

Importantly, we know from studies of digital media use in everyday life that we cannot separate what happens on-screen from what happens off it. Thinking about practices doesn't just involve what we do onscreen or online, but what we do off screen and how the on/off screen and the on/ offline intersect. Studies for example have explored:

- how 'being together' in classrooms often involves a mesh of on-/off-screen activity (Burnett, 2015b);
- how going for a night out with friends is likely to be patterned by a range of digitally mediated and face-to-face interactions (Davies, 2014);
- how playing in virtual worlds may involve operating across a range of on and off screen networks (Leander & McKim, 2003).

The critical networks model encourages us to reflect not just on what we do on-screen – as if we can distance ourselves from digital environments and act objectively within or on them – but to explore how what we do on- and off-screen are entangled with each other, sometimes supplementing or shaping one another and at other times contradicting, conflicting and disrupting. With this in mind, we might reflect on how some of the following might (or might not) be advantageous and empowering for the learners we work with:

- circulating information or sharing opinions that relate to media consumption (e.g. soap operas, videogames, books, movies, celebrity tweets);
- canvassing wider opinion, seeking advice or support (e.g. social issues, personal difficulties, technical problems, crowdsourcing);
- coordinating action on social or political issues (e.g. petitioning, environmental action, smart mobs, demonstrations);
- enhancing personal and family relationships (e.g. sharing minutiae, emotions, jokes, coordinating arrangements, social events);
- sharing and developing occupational or educational activity (e.g. announcements, news and updates, backchannelling).

(From Burnett & Merchant, 2011: 52–3)

Reflecting on what we are doing and how we are positioned by ourselves and others can, we suggest, lead powerfully to consideration of what *might* we be doing and how *could* we position ourselves in ways that are advantageous to ourselves or others. This advantage may work out in different ways: for example, increasing individuals' life chances, enhancing civic engagement, empowerment through collaboration and participation, making a positive contribution to the wider community, or recognising and responding to diverse identities and viewpoints.

Of course we cannot know the kinds of communicative practices that might emerge in the future. Things may begin look and feel very different. Use of virtual reality, for example, is widely predicted to increase exponentially over the next few years, and this may add nuance to existing discussions about how we engage with criticality as distinctions between the 'actual' and 'virtual' continue to blur. Such developments will raise new kinds of questions about what we can do, who we can be and which networks we belong to, and how children might put all this to their own and others' advantage.

Summary

This chapter has explored why it is important for children to consider critically the digital media they encounter and the practices in which they engage. We have explored some practical ways of encouraging children to reflect on how they position themselves and are positioned by others, and to make or rework texts to reflect alternative possibilities and experiences. We have argued that, building on existing models of critical literacy, critical literacy for a digital age involves encouraging children to think critically and creatively about how they present themselves on-screen, how far they are empowered (or not) by the communities they participate in, and how broader social, economic, political and commercial interests are served (or not) by what they do and by the digital texts and environments they use (Black & Reich, 2013 Burnett & Merchant, 2011; Carrington & Hodgetts, 2010).

QUESTIONS FOR REFLECTION

1. When you next search online, reflect on the advertisements that appear as you do so (e.g. recommended purchases). Consider how your search history is influencing what you see when you search.

2. Use the Critical Networks Model to map your own use of digital media. Which practices do you engage in? Which networks do you access? What do these enable you to do (individually or with others)? And how are you positioned (by yourself and others) through these different practices?

3. How might you encourage children to reflect on their practices, identities and networks? How far are their practices advantageous to them (or not), e.g. following interests or in terms of social, civic or political participation? What role do you think teachers should play in supporting advantageous participation?

10

PROMOTE COLLABORATION AROUND AND THROUGH TEXTS IN NEGOTIATING MEANING

Learning about new media is not just about doing things with technology. It is also about doing things with others. Recent studies provide rich insights into the ways in which children and young people collaborate and interact on and around screens. While encouraging such collaborations, we need to be alert to the complex ways in which such interactions are managed and support children to take up such opportunities with confidence.

This chapter will:

- examine the possibilities of on- and off-screen collaboration

- consider the learning potential in co-production using digital tools

- explore the professional challenges of facilitating different kinds of collaborative work.

Scientists remain puzzled after they found a series of strange markings in a local park. The unusual markings were found over the weekend at Heathlands Park, Halfway, which remained closed for a number of hours. Violet Parker, of Halfway said 'They looked like burn marks in the grass. They were large circles, with smaller circles around each side.' The 10-year-old, who was walking through the park after visiting friends, reported she had never seen anything like it before.

Scientists, who are examining photographs of the strange markings, are also studying what appear to be footprints close to the large, mysterious circles. The footprints, which were covered in an unusual green liquid, were found.

(Continued)

(Continued)

Comments:

Amy
I think a aliens space ship crashed or landed on the ground leavin strange markings ☺ x
Dylan
A metor crashed in heathlands park and mellted the mettal.

This news feature was written by class teacher Rob Hobson and his 10-year-old pupils as part of a project that involved making productive use of mobile technologies in school literacy work (DeFT Project, 2013). Under Rob's guidance, the children designed a treasure hunt around the theme of a science fiction narrative located in a park which was within easy walking distance of the school. Online clues were provided through QR codes hidden around the park, and these were later followed by other groups of children from his school. As they discovered these clues children were asked to leave comments on a blog, and as they followed the trail they began to piece together a story of their own making. The use of mobile devices and QR codes made it possible for children to explore the physical environment together, while simultaneously collaborating and interacting with online material. As Rob observed, this took technology out of the usual confines of the school and, by drawing on his own interest in geo-tagging, he was able to plan a rich and different sort of learning experience for his class and the school as a whole.

This project work involved a variety of different kinds of collaboration. In the first instance, Rob and his class worked together on designing the trail and its associated theme, and then, in smaller groups, the children developed clues, created text (such as the news feature above), found images and created video material. Later in the process they helped younger children to follow these clues when they visited the park and encouraged them to post their comments and reactions online, thereby creating a shared text out of the experience. Like the alternate reality game referred to in Chapter 6, collaboration therefore also involved working across age-groups within the school.

Working together

One unfortunate by-product of the drive for greater accountability in education has been the importance accorded to individual achievement. Although ensuring individual progress is a key function of any education system, children and young people also need to learn to work together. In fact, the so-called 'soft skills' of collaboration, negotiation and group problem-solving happen to be highly valued 21st century skills and they are central to employability (Andrews & Higson, 2008). And, of course, since learning is essentially a social endeavour (Gee, 2004), this sort of work builds on a well-established tradition of group work and peer learning that is still valued by many teachers and in many schools.

However, working together is probably harder to design and organise than many commentators have suggested (see Gillies & Boyle, 2010), and although many primary school classrooms have group seating arrangements, individual activity on common tasks is often the norm. Although evidence for the social and cognitive benefits of collaborative learning is persuasive (see, for example, Tolmie et al., 2010) it is not surprising, given the current emphasis on direct teaching and individual assessment, that a report commissioned by the Cambridge Primary Review Trust found that primary school children usually sit in groups but are rarely required to interact or work together as a group (Blatchford et al., 2013).

One might expect this emphasis on individual work to carry over into the use of new technology, which is often conceived of as a solitary activity. Indeed early reactions to children's use of computers at home and school were often flavoured by a moral panic that saw the use of digital technology as a lone, socially isolating phenomenon (Livingstone, 2009). But over time, perceptions have begun to shift as a wealth of research studies have shown how children's leisure and educational uses of technology often involve side-by-side collaborative activity as well as online interaction. Examples include Davidson and colleagues' studies of children's interactions with peers and family members around PCs and tablets at home (Davidson, 2009, 2012) and Ito et al.'s analysis of the various ways in which children and young people collaborate through social media, gaming and special interest groups (2009). Indeed, Ching-Ting, Li and Chin-Chung's (2014) review of studies of technology and young children identified social interaction as a recurrent theme in children's online play.

As technology has become more accessible and more portable, previous constraints – such as having to sit in front of monitors or allocate teaching groups into specialist rooms – have softened. As our opening case study shows, along with many other examples in this book, the possibilities for integrating technology into ongoing learning activity have never been so rich.

Digital collaboration

Certain domains of economic and cultural life have a long tradition of cross-regional and transnational collaboration. The flow of goods and ideas is, of course, a central feature of social life and human communication. The scale, speed and reach of the interactions that lie at the heart of this have all increased with the rapid rise of internet-based communication. Although it pays to be cautious about celebrating the connected world of 'globalisation' (see Burnett et al., 2014), digital collaboration has changed the ways in which many of us work. For example, academic life, with its long history of transnational dialogue now thrives on forms of digital communication that facilitate relatively smooth and immediate connection between researchers with shared interests working across geographical boundaries and time zones through the use of email, videoconferencing, online repositories, learning platforms and so on.

Everyday uses of new technology, and particularly those that feature in the lives of children and young people, are often recreational and they are more likely to involve friends and family members. But it is also true that some children will have experience of collaborating with others in online communities such as those related to videogaming and similar interests (Pearce & Artemesia, 2010). Studies that champion the notion that new technologies can transform education often rest on claims for the benefits of connected (i.e. social and collaborative) learning. However, successful and sustained work on digital collaboration in school contexts has rarely been documented.

Projects that have sought to generate opportunities for students to collaborate with those in other locations have found that such collaboration is not straightforward and that such work needs to be underpinned by a strong ethical dimension. Stornaiuolo (2016) describes a project through which teenagers from India, South Africa and the United States shared digital artefacts including photos, essays and short films with a view to exchanging perspectives and engaging in dialogue. The teachers found it challenging to facilitate online interactions given that there were often conflicting opinions which brought questions of power, privilege, culture and difference to the fore. Such differences provided a powerful starting point, however, for reflective work and students were encouraged to respond to each other's digital artefacts through remixing them, generating digital artefacts that were effectively co-produced by students in different locations. While such projects are less common with younger learners, many schools have used digital platforms as sites for children to share responses and reflections. Kate Cosgrove, for example, provided frequent opportunities for her class of 6–7-year-olds to post on a class blog (DeFT Project, 2013). On one occasion, after creating observational drawings of flowers using the *Brushes* app, children shared their comments on the experience. Comments posted included:

What I liked best on the I pads was where we get to go on the colour wheel and pick a colour and the other bit was where we get to draw the flower and pick how fat or thin you want your brush to be ☺

I enjoyed the different brushes you use on the ipads and the delicate touches you can use whenj painting on the ipad, ☺

I liked it because you could use your fingers to draw. ☺

Connected learning (Penuel & DiGacomo, 2017) is one approach that has championed the cause of collaboration as a 21st century competence. It is based on interest-driven learning that involves collaboration with peers and mentors:

> Rather than frame our task as improving individual competitiveness, we feel it is important to address the overall health of communities and learning writ large, centring our values on equity, full participation and collective contribution.

> *(Ito et al., 2013: 34)*

Connected learning frequently makes use of digital media to achieve its goals of participation and collaboration, either through interaction with peers and mentors or by using technology to produce 'original artifacts for outside audiences' (Penuel & DiGacomo, 2017: 132). In another university college students worked in *Minecraft* with children to explore coding, engineering, game design and digital citizenship (http://connectedcamps. com/). In these projects the young children were encouraged to take the lead, supported by the more knowledgeable mentors.

Co-constructing texts

The kinds of collaborations described above involve negotiating perspectives or activities *through* digital media or working together *around* a screen or device. A third kind of collaboration – perhaps the one which most challenges the current focus on individual outcomes in schools – involves children working together to *co-construct* texts on-screen. In everyday life, many people are familiar with using applications such as *Google Docs* to jointly create and edit shared documents, and recognise how such opportunities enable people to pool, challenge and extend one another's ideas, even when working at a distance. Often this means they achieve something more, and/or more quickly, than they could have done alone. The process of collaborative text creation offers considerable potential for supporting learning through: exchanging perspectives and peer review; gathering, collating and sharing information; as well as developing ideas and imagining new possibilities together (e.g. see Chapter 8 on fanfiction).

Perhaps the most well-known example of a co-constructed text is *Wikipedia*, the continuously updated online encyclopaedia that relies on the expertise – and monitoring – of contributors worldwide for its content and accuracy. Whether you align with its critics who decry gender bias in its contents and lack of checks and balances in its production or its advocates who celebrate its role in the democratisation of knowledge, most would agree that it serves as a compelling example of how the production and distribution of knowledge has changed in recent years. If learners are to engage critically with such sites, and perhaps even more importantly be equipped to engage in co-production of knowledge themselves, then they need experience as critical and creative co-constructers of text.

There are many examples of such co-construction in the chapters of this book – Chris Bailey's Minecraft Club for example (see Chapter 7), in which children co-created an imaginary town in which they played and, as they did so, produced other digital artefacts (books, buildings, tools, etc.) for peers to take up in different ways. And examples of the use of wikis for collaboration in primary schools are growing. Woo et al. (2013), for instance, describes how primary children collaborated using a wiki hosted by *pbwiki*, and concludes that collaborating in this way can provide a useful context for peer feedback and for engagement with writing as a process.

However, as explored in Chapter 5, the process of collaborating on-screen is complex, inflected as it is by a multitude of material, social, historical and cultural factors. Moreover, navigating the co-production of shared text can involve subtle and sensitive work, and when these negotiations happen on-screen at a distance, this can be particularly challenging. Our own experiences of writing collaboratively highlight the importance of:

- being prepared to share work in progress, take risks and try things out, even if they ultimately don't work out;
- willingness to let go one's own ideas or words when they don't work for the joint piece;
- switching between taking a lead and running with others' ideas;
- if a collaborator's contribution doesn't seem to make sense, taking time to explore what the collaborator was trying to achieve (rather than revising or reworking immediately);
- sensitivity to others' ideas and their 'ways with words';
- taking stock of the direction the whole piece may be heading rather than just your individual contribution.

These challenges adopt a particular nuance when children are asked to collaborate on-screen while co-present in class. In one class for example, as part of a project on alternative energy, children used *Google Docs* to collaborate to produce a single table that listed reasons for and against building wind turbines. The children worked in groups, each with a laptop. The teacher asked them to use a selection of pre-selected internet sites to research possible arguments and counter-arguments and note these on the

table. Anyone could amend the content at any time. The table was also pro-
jected onto the interactive whiteboard at the front of the class.

In this example, we can see how the children – new to working together
on a shared document – faced many of the challenges faced by adult col-
laborators – of what to do when someone posts something you feel doesn't
fit, for example, and how you react when someone else deletes what you
have just done. All this was intensified by possible technical glitches and an
unfamiliarity with the process. Moreover, as we see in the second half of the
vignette, sometimes it just does not seem logical to communicate online. It
makes much more sense to talk with those who are with you, to collaborate
face to face.

> There was a sense of urgency as the children set to work and they seemed
> keen to complete the task by the end of the lesson. As they did so, however,
> they faced a number of frustrations and challenges. Some of these related to
> negotiating composition around a shared laptop: given that only one person
> could type, children often obscured the screen for the rest of the group as
> they leaned across to add to or change the text. Other challenges arose
> because they were composing a shared document: one group was surprised
> to see text appearing on the interactive whiteboard and then realised that this
> was because another group was typing; some contributions were typed in and
> then apparently deleted by another group; sometimes, as one group saved
> their contributions, the text disappeared from the other screens.
>
> At one point, the phrase 'block the radar' appeared on the screen in front
> of a group I was observing. This caused a stir on the table – the children did
> not know what 'block the radar' meant. Realising that someone else in the
> class had typed this, one boy wandered round until he found the group
> responsible and asked them to explain. A boy from the second group stood
> up to do so: facing the other boy, he used his arms to represent the turbine
> and mimed how radar could be blocked by the moving blades. This occurred
> in the (usually unoccupied) space between the tables. Once happy with the
> explanation the boy returned to his original table. As he got there, a new
> suggestion appeared on screen: 'Easy to demolish'. Again he went on a hunt
> to find out who had written this. This time he seemed more interested in
> finding the identity of the author than the meaning of the comment.
>
> *(Cited in Burnett, 2011b)*

Making the world together

In addition to the close collaborations with known others described above,
co-construction may also manifest in a more distributed, wide-ranging
coordination of individual activity. Various commentators have highlighted

how such opportunities can enable new forms of civic engagement that enable people to learn from and with each other in myriad ways. Facer (2011), for example, describes how Bristol citizens were 'to digitally "tag" the city with an idea, an experience or a virtual reality' (a story of past memories or events, for example, or an imagined reworking of a particular site), just as Rob's class did in their local park, albeit on a rather smaller scale. Working with older students on the Write4Change project, Stornaiuolo, Hull and Hall (2017) have helped establish an international online network of teachers, young people and other partners through which participants can share perspectives using a range of digital media. Such work has the potential to strengthen ties between previously unknown others, provide opportunities to express solidarity and to engage in social activism. While there are fewer examples of this kind of work in primary schools, the use of digital media to support civic engagement has much to offer a critical literacy pedagogy. These ideas and approaches are explored more fully in the next chapter.

Summary

In this chapter we have explored the possibilities and challenges associated with enabling children to make texts together, exploring issues and questions related to collaboration on-screen and off. We have explored the rich possibilities generated through such collaborations but also highlighted how such work needs careful facilitation. Finally we have signalled how online collaboration may open out opportunities for children to participate more actively in the world around them.

QUESTIONS FOR REFLECTION

1. Reflect on your own communicative practices over the course of a day. How far are these individual and how far collaborative? At what points (if any) do you collaborate and how do you achieve this (e.g. which apps or programs do you use)? Which factors make any collaboration easier? Or more difficult?

2. Review a recent classroom literacy activity. Which opportunities for collaboration did you integrate within the activity? Were there other opportunities you could have provided? How might digital media have supported these?

11

MAKING THE
FUTURE TOGETHER

This chapter will:

- argue that addressing 21st century literacies in primary education requires a flexibility and creativity that can best be generated when educators are given opportunities to work collaboratively in risk-free environments

- explore how the worldwide Maker Movement (Hatch, 2014) may provide inspiration for such collaborative work, and reflect on our own experiences of working with teachers in 21st Century Literacies Maker Circles

- consider how the nine principles for digital media outlined in our Charter might usefully underpin *teachers'* collaborative work in promoting 21st century literacies

- argue for drawing on qualitative research in informing practice in this ever-changing area.

In her project, Jeannie Bulman coordinated the work of four primary schools in Lincolnshire. Inspired by reading about plans to explore Mercury, her group of teachers decided on collaborative work that would involve children in their classes in imaginative exploration and storying of their own. It was decided that each school would adopt a different role in an unfolding narrative. One class took on the role of NASA, another class were astronauts recruited to the mission, while the other two were inhabitants of Earth and Mercury respectively. NASA initiated the work by sending a mission brief to the astronauts, who designed characters with different backgrounds and skills and then interviewed them. Meanwhile, the Earth group researched space travel and planned to create media coverage about the expensive and controversial plans. The Mercury group, unaware, of all this, were busy building alien characters particularly suited to the conditions of their distant planet. The imaginary

(Continued)

(Continued)

space flight was documented in a short video which combined found film footage with animation. Eventually, the astronauts' approach to Mercury was announced by email, and the Mercury inhabitants sent back pictures of themselves (as aliens) using the Morfo app. These images were then sent on to the NASA and Earth groups. Astronauts used drawing apps to share their views of the landscape of Mercury. In a final narrative twist it became apparent that the mission's real intent was invasion and colonisation to escape from a polluted Earth and not just a simple case of scientific exploration!

This project developed cross-school collaboration using a range of media, as children created plots and sub-plots in an open-ended narative. Email and *Edmodo* were important ways of sustaining the collaboration, but other digital and non-digital media were woven in at appropriate points. In part, the story was driven by children's interests, research and exploration. Rather than being outcomes driven, the teachers encouraged playfulness, improvisation and experimentation, providing a contrast to some of the more conventional practices that have become common place in classrooms in the UK. In doing this, the work incorporated many of the principles listed in the Charter.

Throughout this book we have explored these principles, each arising from an analysis of literacies in everyday life, and we have reflected on how they might usefully inform our planning for using digital media in the classroom. To recap, these principles – introduced in Chapter 1 and framed as principles for pedagogy and curriculum in the Charter for 21st Century Literacies (Burnett et al., 2014) – can be summarised as follows:

- Acknowledge the changing nature of meaning making
- Recognise and build on children's linguistic, social and cultural repertoires
- Acknowledge diverse modes and media
- Recognise the affective, embodied and material dimensions of meaning making
- Encourage improvisation and experimentation
- Use playful pedagogies
- Create opportunities to work with the provisionality of digital media
- Provide contexts that facilitate criticality
- Promote collaboration around and through texts in negotiating meaning

In our opening vignette, we see how many of these themes can intersect in classrooms – classrooms where space has been made for communicative practices that draw on the digital in the context of motivating and meaningful work, often led by the children, and where opportunities are seized for communicating with others beyond the classroom walls. In this example, Jeannie's teacher group was not simply looking for opportunities to accommodate digital technologies within *existing* practice – letting children type rather than write, for example – but worked with digital media in ways that generated new kinds of possibilities for them to connect, try things out and collaborate. Not only did they use blogging, drawing apps, video and email, they were also involved in pencil-and-paper tasks like drafting newspaper reports and sketching aliens. But the project work also meant that they had to research space travel, find out about the landscape and atmosphere on Mercury – one class arranged a visit to the National Space Centre – and so on. In its final phase children also looked into environmental concerns and the ethics of investing precious resources in space exploration.

However, the Charter is not intended as a comprehensive list of the kinds of things that teachers need to pay attention to when planning for digital media and responding to the changing nature of literacy. There are other frameworks that can provide support with this process. For example, practitioners have successfully adapted Luke and Freebody's '4 Resources Model' for the digital age, building on its proposals for framing literacy curricula to support literacy learners in four 'roles': as code breakers, meaning makers, text users and text analysts (Freebody & Luke, 1990). Serafini (2011) extends this model to encompass the reading of multimodal texts, thinking instead of the roles of navigator, interpreter, designer and interrogator. The New London Group's 'Pedagogy of Multiliteracies' – and its repertoire of situated practice, overt instruction, critical framing and transformed practice – continues to be influential in some countries in reworking literacy provision for the 21st century (Cope & Kalantzis, 2000). What the Charter does highlight, however, are some principles for literacy provision that are particularly relevant given the fluid, mobile and participatory ways in which digital media are now used in everyday life.

In writing these chapters, we have often reflected on the *familiarity* of many of the ideas we explore. In Chapter 2 we explored continuities between digital and print literacies, and we could trace similar continuities between the principles we propose in the Charter and long-established approaches to literacy provision. Very few of the themes are new, and many of their implications for pedagogy – such as working with what children know, going with the flow, ensuring children reach real audiences, and encouraging opportunities for peer review – echo those we have been arguing for throughout our educational careers, long before the digital made its way into classrooms. They are the kinds of approaches that have underpinned much seminal work in drama in education, writers' workshops and critical pedagogy (e.g. see O'Neill, 1995; Graves, 1983; Janks, 2010).

So what is new here? Why might it be worth revisiting these ideas for the digital age?

The same old story: some familiar issues

Readers will have very different experiences of experimenting with digital media in their own lives, both personally and professionally. We hope, however, that the ideas and practices described in this book will have chimed with existing practice, helped bolster the rationale for why some practices are important, and perhaps provided some inspiration for other approaches to explore in the future. At the same time, we recognise that integrating digital media into contemporary classroom practice can be challenging. There are a number of reasons for this.

For many teachers, the logistical challenges of working online and on-screen can be a source of ongoing frustration. The kinds of creative and collaborative projects described in this book can all too easily be thwarted by:

- scarcity of resources
- faulty equipment
- drained batteries or inaccessible power supplies
- unreliable internet connections
- procedures for installing apps or booking equipment
- complex and individualised log-in codes
- unfamiliar hardware and software
- lack of available technical support
- e-safety policies and practices (e.g. firewalls) that with the best of intentions frustrate attempts to push classroom learning beyond classroom walls.

While many teachers are confident users of digital media in their own lives, sometimes adding technology into the mix can seem to over-complicate the already complicated task of primary teaching. Moreover, as we explore in Chapter 1, national curriculum and assessment frameworks do not always provide much of a warrant for integrating digital media, and when they do, the focus may be on technicist and functional uses rather than the creative and critical dimensions we have explored in this volume.

Of course teachers have leeway to enact curriculum as they wish and many have found ways of working with digital media within existing frameworks (Monkhouse et al., 2017). However, the free-flowing, spontaneous approaches we have recommended do not sit easily alongside the highly structured literacy provision that exists in many countries. As studies of student teachers' perpections of the use of digital media have suggested, working in this way may – for some – feel at odds with other aspects of what they feel is expected of them as professionals (Burnett, 2011a; Nikolopoulou & Gialamas, 2015).

A significant organisational challenge for teachers we have worked with has been how to convince senior leaders in their schools that it is important to dedicate time to the work, and this has often involved careful readings of relevant curriculum frameoworks – in England this means reading across the English *and* Computing programmes of study (DfE, 2013). Often though, teachers have had to be opportunistic in carrying out project work (such as using time freed up through the cancellation of an event, staff absence or a necessary divergence from what had been planned). They have also had to be creative in their use of space and resources, working from their insider knowledge of when particular rooms or equipment such as iPads or laptops were not being used by others. In other words, making time for digital media may well involve being both strategic and tactical in approach. Nevertheless, the apparent contradictions between statutory frameworks and the kinds of approaches advocated in this book are difficult to navigate. Such challenges are exacerbated by difficulties in accessing information and guidance about what might be possible and how it might be worthwhile. Some of the reasons for this are explored in the next section.

Engaging with research on digital media: a word about 'evidence-based practice'

In recent years, much has been made of 'evidence-based practice', of drawing on 'hard' evidence of what works in making decisions about educational innovation and investment. We see this, for example, in the 'What Works' movement and specifically the work of the influential Education Endowment Foundation in the UK (EEF, 2017), which generates and synthesises evidence on interventions that are effective in terms of evidence gathered from randomised control trials. Recommendations for 'effective' approaches that draw on this kind of evidence have emphasised priorities for pedagogy such as providing clear objectives and assessment criteria and ensuring children have opportunities for feedback against these criteria and to reflect on what they have learned. Such approaches are attractive to many educators and school leaders as they appear to parcel up learning into bite-size chunks that are manageable for teachers and children. This process also makes it possible to track 'observable progress' which, in England, has been a key focus for Ofsted inspections. The logic here is that if children know what they are supposed to learn, and know what learning looks like, then they are more likely to focus on the things that matter. Advocates of such approaches cite studies that have linked their use to marked improvements in children's attainment, for example in the research linked to formative assessment (Wiliam, 2011) and metacognition (Hattie, 2008).

In this book we certainly do not want to argue against the value of such strategies in a teaching repertoire. What we do suggest, however, is that many of the approaches and orientations that have an important part to play in literacy pedagogy are simply not measurable, and consequently are very unlikely to surface through research that foregrounds 'hard' evidence. There are a number of reasons for this.

First, as is evident in many of the examples cited in this book, many valuable insights into using digital media in classrooms derive from detailed studies of individual projects, projects unique to the context in which they took place, and developed through the collective efforts of teachers and children in particular local circumstances. Their success relies on the intersection of complex sets of social, cultural and material factors, relating, for example, to resources, relationships and passions. While such projects may exemplify how the principles we explore have been embedded in practice, and the kinds of learning opportunities generated as a result, they do not have the reproducibility needed for randomised controlled trials, and do not generate straightforward cause–effect relationships about the impact of certain pedagogies on attainment.

Second, as explored in the previous chapter, the communicative landscape is constantly changing: new practices are emerging, and what might be seen as 'effective' is up for debate. The assessment practices associated with standardised assessment, for example, often used as part of the 'evidence base' in randomised controlled trials and quasi-experimental studies, simply cannot keep pace with this shifting landscape. Moreover, much of what the chapters of this book have shown to be significant to children's media use – feeling, movement, improvisation, and so on – are tricky, if not impossible, to capture and quantify. If we rely on 'hard evidence' to inform our decision-making, if we focus only on what is measurable, there is a risk of narrowing our provision in ways that miss the creative, critical dimensions of literacy, that miss some of the value of what is being done. If we place high stakes on measurement, then there is a risk that creative and critical dimensions disappear from practice altogether, or at least take a back seat. Arguably this is what has happened in England in recent years as the measurement of literacy through national testing arrangments has led to a focus primarily on what is measurable (Moss, 2012).

Learning about and with digital media may require us to think more broadly about the kind of research we use in developing practice. Qualitative studies that provide rich descriptions of practices within and beyond classroms and teacher-led research that involves careful reflection on children's literacies in classroom contexts may provide more generative ways forward for groups of teachers. In such contexts, reflection and working with others are likely to provide rich opportunities for professional learning. Rather than using evidence to inform practice – an approach that has been criticised for overplaying the extent to which practices can be portable from one context to another (Wrigley, 2016) – we might focus on *thinking with* evidence, using evidence as the starting point for professional discussion, reflection and action. As such we might draw on a range of evidence, not just quantitative, but stories of practice, media artefacts produced by children, and what children show and tell us about what is important to them. Shifting the gaze from measurable impacts to what children are doing highlights different kinds of questions, issues and possibilities for the classroom, questions, issues and possibilities that can perhaps best be explored by teachers working – or making – provision for digital media together.

Making together

Some of the most compelling and innovative work involving digital media has emerged from projects designed to bring teachers together. In recent years it has become commonplace for groups of schools to work together to develop practice often linked to identified priorities, and such collaboration is increasingly viewed as a central part of a teacher's professional role. In England this has often involved schools belonging to academy chains and/ or teaching school alliances. Such groupings may well provide rich ground for developing the use of digital media, as may more serendipitous exchanges of practice through Teachmeets and social media. Carpenter and Krutka (2014), for example, documented the many ways in which teachers use *Twitter* to support their professional development, sharing resources and garnering views, for example, reflecting on practice and keeping up to date with educational issues. The opportunities we want to showcase in this chapter, however, are more sustained than those generated through social media and one-off gatherings, but less structured than those often generated through existing school groupings.

In thinking about how teachers can collaborate to explore the integration of digital media, the loosely defined and increasingly popular 'Maker Movement' provides some inspiration. In recent years the Maker Movement has gathered momentum across the globe, taking the form of makerspaces in libraries, schools and other community venues where people come together to make, create and experiment with materials and share experiences (Hatch, 2014). Makerspaces are often resourced to support activities such as coding, electronics, robotics, and so on, but can just as easily involve resources like fabric, wood, cardboard and Lego blocks. While many have a science, technology or mathematics focus, increasingly makerspaces are springing up that support media making: creating films, designing games, making photo documentaries and so on (Peppler, Halverson & Kafai, 2016), and online communities such as MakerBridge (http://makerbridge.si.umich.edu/)

facilitate cross fertilisation between groups. They are places designed to foster curiosity, collaboration, interest and 'tinkering' (DiGiacomo, Gutierrez & Schwartz, 2013).

Our own work with colleagues in what we call '21st Century Literacies Maker Circles' attempts to bring similar principles to bear on creative digital media projects in primary schools. The recipe is simple enough. A cross-school group of teachers meets together to devise a project that involves children in some kind of exchange in a digital space. This digital space could be generated through any program or app that allows the children to share views or ideas – *Skype*, for example, a site like *Padlet*, or a virtual environment like *Minecraft*. In our experience teachers have tended to stay with something that they're already using in school, like *Edmodo*. Contributions may take various forms such as video, photo, comment, even scanned drawing or hand-written pieces. The aim here isn't to develop teachers' technical skills or promote the use of new software (although that may well happen as the project unfolds). Instead it is about developing contexts for drawing on and building children's communication repertoires, and exploring the kinds of literacies that are produced as a result. Driving questions are:

- How might we support different kinds of collaborations? And how can we enable individuals and groups to collaborate in ways that are empowering to themselves and others?
- How might we encourage different kinds of 'makings'?
- And how can we enable use of a diversity of resources?

Examples of projects might include:

- Children working across schools to construct an imagined space to generate characters and events that build into a shared emerging story. In Chapter 6 we describe how an imagined street was constructed between two schools. The street existed partly in what children posted online – character descriptions, estate agent's brochures, maps – but also developed a life of its own as it surfaced in the stories children wove around it, told in written narratives and television news broadcasts all posted on a blog.
- Developing responses to an issue or event and then sharing these with other schools on a shared platform and deciding as a group how to respond.
- The mysterious disappearance of objects from one classroom that then appear in another school – with children collaborating online to deduce what has happened.
- Children in each class presented with a problem – connected with the local environment for example – creating a solution which they then share, critique and develop across schools.

All of these projects are typified by playfulness, an openness to build on each others' ideas, contributions and creative acts, rather than necessarily collaborating towards a fixed predetermined outcome. Rather than arriving at a fixed plan, the idea is to follow the children's interests and respond to what emerges as the children start to engage. The maker circle approach is designed to work with the principles outlined in the Charter. Importantly, however, the process of teacher collaboration also reflects the Charter's principles: it draws, for example, on teachers' shared expertise, their willingness to improvise, and the energy and inspiration derived from being together (see Table 11.1). We have found that working in this way can also provide moral support and encouragement for teacher participants even if current curriculum and assessment frameworks provide little direction or support. Rather than being driven by the anticipated judgements of external evaluators such as Ofsted, participants can work together to review the worth of what they are doing.

Table 11.1 Applying the Charter principles to teachers' activity

Principles underpinning children's activity	Principles underpinning teachers' activity
Building on children's experiences	Drawing on and exchanging teachers' experiences – of digital media use in own life and as teachers, of teaching across the curriculum, and of literacy teaching (regardless of whether digital media are used)
Using diverse modes and media	Using digital media to manage the collaboration – social media, email, sharing of resources, etc.
Enabling children to set the agenda	Teachers taking charge of when the project will be initiated and unfold
Revisiting, reviewing and responding	Supporting each other to evaluate what enables children's use of digital media and what gets in the way
Focusing on what matters in the moment	Teachers responding to what children do
Making texts together	Making the project together across schools
Facilitating criticality	Reflecting on how their own work as teachers is framed by policy and power and how they might re-frame this
Encouraging improvisation and experimentation	Encouraging one another in risk-taking and tinkering with literacy provision
Acknowledging the changing nature of literacy	Interpreting curriculum in ways that acknowledge changing nature of literacy

Worldwide, many other projects have sought to work in a similar manner: Knobel and Kalman's (2016) book, *New Literacies and Teacher Learning: Professional Learning and the Digital Turn* for example, documents multiple ways in which teachers have collaborated in developing new literacies in school; Comber and Kamler's project developing 'turnaround pedagogies' involved pairing newly qualified and veteran teachers to reflect on children's learning together and devise projects that built on children's media interests (Comber & Kamler, 2005); and Lockerington et al.'s work with a group of teachers over several years generated a safe space for 'learning, planning and sharing' (Lockerington et al., 2016). Like these other educators and researchers we wanted to develop opportunities for teachers to work collaboratively and take risks together, in many ways echoing the kinds of collaboration that happen in affinity groups online (see Gee, 2004). Such opportunities, we hope, not only help generate motivating and productive opportunities for using digital media in classrooms, but give teachers a chance to try things out and provide space for developing pedagogies that run counter to dominant models of teaching and learning. Perhaps they even bolster teachers' confidence in challenging some of these models. As Knobel and Kalman write:

> Playing, experimenting and mucking around help develop a critical stance towards taken-as-normal asusmptions about the world and how it 'works' and such experiences give teachers something to compare and contrast against over-standardised, textbook-driven, content-centred, transmissive pedagogies. This kind of open-ended exploration is time-consuming and somewhat erratic but usefully opens up space for important questions about curriculum and lesson planning, deep learning, and conceptions of learning as linear, controllable and measurable.
>
> *(Knobel & Kalman, 2016: 16)*

Importantly, playful and productive – maybe even transformative – uses of digital media do not necessarily rely on a great deal of technical skill on the part of the teacher. Indeed, sometimes those teachers who are most creative and innovative are those who have a passion not so much for using digital media but for creativity and communication more widely. In their study of teachers' uses of gaming in the classroom, for example, Beavis, Dezuanni and O'Mara (2017) describe how one 'non-gamer' Year 1 teacher gradually found ways of integrating games more creatively into her practice with her class as she tried things out, watched the children and responded to what they did. She moved from quite structured use of games to reinforce existing learning objectives through to games as enrichment, through to far more open-ended possibilities. Partly because of her own lack of confidence with games such as *Minecraft*, she encouraged children to take the lead, and these student-centred pedagogies supported opportunities for deep engagement.

So what's new?

At the start of this chapter we asked why it might be important to return to some familiar themes in education when thinking about digital media. We proposed that it is important to work with the diversity of experience that children bring to school, to be responsive to what they do and to capitalise on the potential for them to engage with others beyond the classroom. In this approach children are encouraged to work playfully, drawing freely on their communicative resources and the materials they have access to, using these resources to create new meanings. We suggest that this helps to broaden their communication repertoires and develops a creative, reflective and critical sensibility which is in step with everyday practices.

The Charter is an attempt to bring together these ways of working in a manageable form, while recognising that – as we explored in our reflections on the opening vignette – the nine principles are inextricably interlinked. The issues explored in the previous two sections go some way to explaining why these are particularly important areas to address *now*. If we try to fit digital media provision within existing frameworks for literacy we will inevitably miss key dimensions that are central to the creative, critical and collaborative uses of digital media that are so central to children's social, civic, political and economic participation in the world around them. This participation is not just dependent on sets of measurable skills and competencies (old or new), but on how uses of digital media work to bring children in relation to others – as members of groups, communities and societies – with implications not just for collective economic well-being but for social, civic and cultural life, and for a socially, politically and environmentally just world. All of this is important for children's future lives but it is also important for their lives now.

What's future-proof?

It would be hard, perhaps impossible, to find an educational approach that is genuinely future-proof. In a way the whole idea runs contrary to notions about using children's interest, available resources and communication repertoires, all of which are constantly in flux. Digital media, and the entire technological revolution that it is connected with, is, as we know, characterised by rapid change. Drones, driverless vehicles, artificial intelligence, virtual reality and nano-technology are as much a part of life as the daily newsfeeds about environmental degradation, mass migration and human conflict, and children have to make sense of this in all its complexity. What is important, in terms of values and ethical behaviour, is how to respond to changing circumstances, to new and emerging issues and dilemmas. Human communication and interaction are, however, key resources and although it is highly likely that media and devices will continue to evolve, children and young people need to be provided with opportunities to understand how they work, to express themselves with confidence and to be critical producers and consumers.

REFERENCES

Alper, M. (2013). Developmentally appropriate new media literacies: supporting cultural competencies and social skills in early childhood education. *Journal of Early Childhood Literacy, 13*(2), 175–196.

Andrews, J. & Higson, H. (2008). Graduate employability 'soft skills' versus 'hard' business knowledge: a European study. *Higher Education in Europe, 33*(4), 411–422.

Appadurai, A. (1996). *Modernity at large: cultural dimensions of globalization.* Minneapolis, MN: University of Minnesota.

Apple, M. (1982) *Education and power.* London: Routledge & Kegan Paul.

Askeland, N. & Maager, E. (2010). Tasting words and letting them hang in the air. *European Early Childhood Education Research Journal, 18*(1), 75–91.

Australian Curriculum and Reporting Authority (ACARA) (2013). *The Australian Curriculum.* Available at: https://australiancurriculum.edu.au/.

Bailey, C. (2016). Free the sheep: improvised song and performance in and around a Minecraft community. *Literacy, 50,* 62–71.

Bailey, C., Burnett, C. & Merchant, G. (2017). Assembling literacies in virtual play. In K. Mills, A. Stornaiuolo, A. Smith & J. Pandya (Eds), *Routledge Handbook of digital writing and literacies in education* (pp. 187–197). New York: Routledge.

Bakhtin, M.M. (1981). *The dialogic imagination: four essays by M.M. Bakhtin* (M. Holquist, Ed.; C. Emerson & M. Holquist, Trans.). Austin, TX: University of Texas Press (original work published 1935).

Barnes, D. (1976). *From communication to curriculum.* Harmondsworth: Penguin.

Barton, D. (2007). *Literacy: an introduction to the ecology of written language* (2nd Edn). London: Routledge.

Barton, D. & Lee, C. (2013). *Language online: investigating digital texts and practices.* London: Routledge.

Barton, D., Hamilton, M. & Ivanic, R. (Eds) (2000). *Situated literacies: reading and writing in context.* London: Routledge.

Bearne, E. (2009). Assessing multimodal texts. In A. Burke & R. Hammett (Eds), *Assessing new literacies: perspectives from the classroom* (pp. 15–33). New York: Peter Lang.

Bearne, E. (2017). Assessing children's written texts. *Literacy, 54*(2), 74–83.

Beavis, C., Dezuanni, M. & O'Mara, J. (2017). *Serious play: literacy, learning and digital games.* London: Routledge.

Black, R. & Reich, S. (2013). A sociocultural approach to exploring virtual worlds. In G. Merchant, J. Gillen, J. Marsh & J. Davies (Eds), *Virtual literacies: interactive spaces for children and young people* (pp. 27–40). New York: Routledge.

Blatchford, P., Hallam, S., Ireson, J.K. & Kutnik, P. (2013), with Creech, A. (2008). Classes, groups and transitions: structures for teaching and learning. *Primary Review Research Briefings*, 9(2).

Boldt, G., Lewis, C. & Leander, K.M. (2015). Moving, feeling, desiring, teaching. *Research in the Teaching of English*, 49, 430–441.

Bourdieu, P. (1992). *Language and symbolic power*. Cambridge: Polity Press.

Brandt, D. (2015). *The rise of writing: redefining mass literacy*. Cambridge: Cambridge University Press.

Brennan, K. (2016). Audience in the service of learning: how kids negotiate attention in an online community of interactive media designers. *Learning, Media and Technology*, 41(2), 193–212.

Broadhead, P. (2004). *Early years play and learning*. London: Routledge.

Buckingham, D. (2003). *Media education: literacy, learning and contemporary culture*. Cambridge: Polity.

Bulman, J. (2017). *Children's reading of film and visual literacy in the primary curriculum*. London: Palgrave.

Burbules, N. (1997). Rhetorics of the web: hyperreading and critical literacy. In I. Snyder (Ed.), *Page to screen: taking literacy into the electronic era* (pp. 102–122). St Leonards, NSW: Allen & Unwin.

Burgess, J. & Green, J. (2013). *YouTube*. Oxford: Wiley.

Burke, A. & Hammett, R. (Eds) (2009). *Assessing new literacies: perspectives from the classroom*. New York: Peter Lang.

Burn, A. (2016). Making machinima: animation, games, and multimodal participation in the media arts. *Learning, Media and Technology*, 41(2), 310–329.

Burn, A. & Parker, D. (2003). *Analysing media texts*. London: Continuum.

Burnett, C. (2011a). Pre-service teachers' digital literacy practices: exploring contingency in identity and digital literacy in and out of educational contexts. *Language and Education*, 25(5), 433–449.

Burnett, C. (2011b). Shifting and multiple spaces in classrooms: an argument for investigating learners' boundary-making around digital networked texts. *Journal of Literacy and Technology*, 12(3), 2–23.

Burnett, C. (2015a). (Im)materialising literacies. In K. Pahl & J. Rowsell (Eds), *The Routledge Handbook of literacy studies*. London: Routledge, pp. 520–531.

Burnett, C. (2015b). Being together in classrooms at the interface of the physical and virtual: implications for collaboration in on/off screen sites. *Learning, Media and Technology*, 41(4), 566–589.

Burnett, C. (2017). The fluid materiality of tablets: examining 'the iPad multiple' in a primary classroom. In C. Burnett, G. Merchant, A. Simpson & M. Walsh (Eds), *Mobile Literacies: The Case of the iPad in Education*. New York: Springer , pp. 15–30.

Burnett, C. (forthcoming). Telling stories out of class: 3 movements in a reach for affect. In K. Leander and C. Ehret (Eds), *Affect in literacy learning and teaching: pedagogies, politics, and coming to know*. New York: Routledge.

Burnett, C. & Bailey, C. (2014). Conceptualising collaboration in hybrid sites: playing Minecraft together and apart in a primary classroom. In C. Burnett,

J. Davies, G. Merchant & J. Rowsell (Eds), *New literacies around the globe: policy and pedagogy* (pp. 50–71). London: Routledge.

Burnett, C. & Merchant, G. (2011). Is there a space for critical literacy in the context of social media? *English Teaching, Practice and Critique, 10*(1), 41–57.

Burnett, C. & Merchant, G. (2014). Points of view: reconceptualising literacies through an exploration of adult and child interactions in a virtual world. *Journal of Research in Reading, 37*(1), 36–50.

Burnett, C. & Merchant, G. (2015). The challenge of 21st-century literacies. *Journal of Adolescent and Adult Literacies, 59*(3), 271–274.

Burnett, C. & Merchant, G. (2016a). Boxes of poison: baroque technique as antidote to simple views of literacy. *Journal of Literacy Research, 48*(3), 258–279.

Burnett, C. & Merchant, G. (2016b). Assembling the virtual. In R. Parry, C. Burnett & G. Merchant, *Literacy, media, technology: past, present and future* (pp. 219–231). London: Bloomsbury.

Burnett, C. & Merchant, G. (2017). The case of the iPad. In C. Burnett, G. Merchant, A. Simpson & M. Walsh (Eds), *The case of the iPad: mobile literacies in education* (pp. 1–14). Singapore: Springer.

Burnett, C. & Myers, J. (2006). Observing children writing on screen: exploring the process of multi-modal composition. *Language and Literacy, 8*(2), 1–30.

Burnett, C. & Wilkinson, J. (2005). Holy lemons! Learning from children's uses of the Internet in out-of-school contexts. *Literacy, 39*(3), 158–165.

Burnett, C., Daniels, K. & Sawka, V. (2016). Teaching strategies. In D. Wyse & S. Rogers (Eds), *A guide to early years and primary teaching* (pp. 125–144). London: Sage.

Burnett, C., Davies, J., Merchant, G. & Rowsell, J. (2014). *New literacies around the globe: policy and pedagogy*. London: Routledge.

Burnett, C., Merchant, G., Simpson, A. & Walsh, M. (Eds) (2017). *The case of the iPad: mobile literacies in education*. Singapore: Springer.

Carpenter, J.P. & Krutka, D.G. (2014). How and why educators use Twitter: a survey of the field. *Journal of Research on Technology in Education, 46*(4), 414–434.

Carrington, V. & Hodgetts, K. (2010). Literacy-lite in BarbieGirls™. *British Journal of Sociology of Education, 31*(6), 671–682.

Cekaite, A. (2005). Language play, a collaborative resource in children's L2 learning. *Applied Linguistics, 26*(2), 169–191.

Ching-Ting, Hsin, Li, M. & Chin-Chung, T. (2014) The influence of young children's use of technology on their learning: a review. *Journal of Educational Technology and Society, 17*(4), 85–99.

Chou, C., Condron, L. & Belland, J.C. (2005). A review of the research on Internet addiction. *Educational Psychology Review, 17*(4), 363–388.

Colvert, A. (2012). 'What is the MFC?' Making and shaping meaning in alternate reality games. In G. Merchant, J. Gillen, J. Marsh & J. Davies (Eds), *Virtual literacies* (pp. 105–125). London: Routledge.

Comber, B. & Kamler, B. (2005). *Turn-around pedagogies: literacy interventions for at-risk students*. Newtown, NSW: Primary English Teaching Association.

Comber, B. & Nixon, H. (2013). Urban renewal, migration and memories: the affordances of place-based pedagogies for developing immigrant students' literate repertoires. *REMIE Multidisciplinary Journal of Educational Research, 3*(1), 42–68.

Cooper, P.M. (2005). Literacy learning and pedagogical purpose in Vivian Paley's 'storytelling curriculum'. *Journal of Early Childhood Literacy*, 5(3), 229–251.

Cope, B. & Kalantzis, M. (Eds) (2000). *Multiliteracies: literacy learning and the design of social futures*. New York: Routledge.

Council for the Curriculum, Examinations and Assessment (CCEA) (2016). *Northern Ireland Curriculum*. Available at: http://ccea.org.uk/curriculum.

Craft, A., Cremin, T., Burnard, P., Dragovic, T. & Chappell, K. (2012). Possibility thinking: culminative studies of an evidence-based concept driving creativity? *Education 3-13*, 41(5), 538–556.

Cranmer, S., Selwyn, J. & Potter, J. (2009). Exploring primary pupils' experiences and understandings of 'e-safety'. *Education and Information Technologies*, 14(2), 127–142.

Curwood, J., Magnifico, A., Lammers, J. (2013). Writing in the wild: Writers' motivation in fan-based affinity spaces. *Journal of Adolescent and Adult Literacy*, 56(8), 677–685.

Curwood, J. (2013). Fan fiction, remix culture, and the Potter Games. In V.E. Frankel (Eds), *Teaching with Harry Potter* (pp. 81–92). Jefferson, NC: McFarland.

Daniels, K. (2016). Magic spells being invisible and flying: young children's expression of the human and superhuman through spatial and material explorations in small world play. Paper Presented at Literacy Research Association conference 2016, Nashville USA (30th Nov–Dec-2nd).

Daniels, K. (2017). Children's engagement with iPads in early years classrooms: exploring peer cultures and transforming practices. In C. Burnett, G. Merchant, A. Simpson & M. Walsh (Eds), *The case of the iPad: mobile literacies in education* (pp. 195–210). Singapore: Springer.

Davidson, C. (2009). Young children's engagement with digital texts and literacies in the home: pressing matters for the teaching of English in the early years of schooling. *English teaching: practice and critique*, 8(3), 36–54.

Davidson, C. (2012). The social organisation of help during young children's use of the computer. *Contemporary Issues in Early Childhood*, 13(3), 187–199.

Davies, J. (2014). (Im)material girls living in (im)material worlds: identity curation through time and space. In C. Burnett, J. Davies, G Merchant & J. Rowsell (Eds), *New literacies around the globe: policy and pedagogy* (pp. 72–87). New York: Routledge.

Davies, J. & Merchant, G. (2009). *Web 2.0 for schools: learning and social participation*. New York: Peter Lang.

DeFT Project (2013). *Digital Futures in Teacher Education*. Available at: http://digitalfutures.realsmart.co.uk/.

DeKoven, B. (2015). Deep fun and the theater of games: an interview with Bernie DeKoven. *American Journal of Play*, 7(2), 137–154.

Deleuze, G. & Guattari, F. (1987). *A thousand plateaus: capitalism and schizophrenia*. London: Continuum.

Department for Education (DfE) (2013). *The National Curriculum for England*. Available at: https://www.gov.uk/government/collections/national-curriculum (accessed 18 April 2018).

Department for Education and Employment (DfEE) (1998). *National Literacy Strategy Framework for Teaching*. London: HMSO.

Dickinson, P., Merchant, G., Burnett, C. & Myers, J. (2006). Digital connections: transforming literacy in the primary school. *Cambridge Journal of Education*, *36*(1), 11–29.

DiGiacomo, D., Gutierrez, K. & Schwartz, L. (2013). *Relationships and tinkering: the generative power of the relationship as a tool for expansive literacies and learning*, Literacy Research Association Conference, Dallas, Texas, 3–6 December.

Dowdall, C. (2009). Impressions, improvisations and compositions: reframing children's text production in social networking sites. *Literacy*, *43*(2), 91–99.

Dyson, A.H. (1993). *Negotiating a Permeable Curriculum: On Literacy, Diversity, and the Interplay of Children's and Teachers' Worlds*. Concept Paper No. 9. Urbana: National Council of Teachers of English.

Dyson, A.H. (2001). Where are the childhoods in childhood literacy? An exploration in outer (school) space. *Journal of Early Childhood Literacy*, *1*(1), 9–39.

Dyson, A.H. (2003). *The brothers and sisters learn to write: popular literacies in childhood and school cultures*. New York: Teachers College Press.

EEF (2017). *Education Endowment Foundation*. Available at: https://education endowmentfoundation.org.uk/about/what-works-network.

Eshet-Alkalai, Y. (2004). Digital literacy: a conceptual framework for survival skills in the digital era. *Journal of Educational Multimedia and Hypermedia*, *13*(1), 93.

Facer, K. (2011). *Learning futures: education, technology and social change*. Abingdon: Routledge.

Fox, N. & Aldred, P. (2017). *Sociology and the new materialism: theory, research, action*. London: Sage.

Freebody, P. & Luke, A. (1990). Literacies programs: debates and demands in cultural context. *Prospect: Australian Journal of TESOL*, *5*(3), 7–16.

Freire, P. (1985). *The politics of education, power and liberation* (Donald Macedo, Trans.). New York: Bergin & Garvey.

Freire, P. & Macedo, D. (1987). *Literacy: reading the word and the world*. South Hadley, MA: Bergin & Garvey.

Friedman, T. (2016). *Thank you for being late: an optimist's guide to thriving in the age of acceleration*. New York: Farrar, Straus and Giroux.

Fuchs, C. (2016). *Social media: a critical introduction*. London: Sage.

Gee, J. (2003). *What videogames have to teach us about learning and literacy*. New York: Palgrave Macmillan.

Gee, J. (2004). *Situated language and learning: a critique of traditional schooling*. London: Routledge.

Gencarelli, T.F. (2006). Neil Postman and the rise of media ecology. In C. Lum (Ed.), *Perspectives on culture, technology, and communication: the media ecology tradition* (pp. 201–253). New York: Hampton.

Giddens, A. (1999). *Runaway World: How Globalisation is Reshaping our Lives*. London: Profile Books.

Gifford, S. (2004). Between the secret garden and the hothouse: children's responses to number focused activities in the nursery. *European Early Childhood Education Research Journal*, *12*(2), 87–102.

Gillen, J. (2014). *Digital literacies*. London: Routledge.

Gillen, J. & Merchant, G. (2013). Contact calls: Twitter as a dialogic social and linguistic practice. *Language Sciences*, *35*, 47–58.

Gillies, R.M. & Boyle, M. (2010). Teachers' reflections on cooperative learning: issues of implementation. *Teaching and Teacher Education*, *26*(4), 933–940.

Gilroy, M. (2010). Higher education migrates to YouTube and social networks. *Education Digest*, *75*(7), 18–22.

Giroux, H. (1994). *Disturbing pleasures*. New York: Routledge.

Grainger, T., Goouch, K. & Lambirth, A. (2005). *Creativity and writing: developing voice and verve in the classroom*. London: Routledge.

Graves, D. (1983). *Writing: teachers and children at work*. Exeter, NH: Heinemann.

Green, B. (2012). Subject-specific literacy, writing and school learning: a revised account. In B. Green and C. Beavis (Eds), *Literacy in 3D: an integrated perspective in theory and practice* (pp. 2–21). Camberwell, Vic.: ACER.

Guardian Newspaper (2017). Primary school children loose marks in Sats test for misshapen commas. *The Guardian*. Available at: https://www.theguardian.com/education/2017/jul/10/primary-school-children-lose-marks-in-sats-tests-for-mis-shaped-commas (accessed 11 July 2017).

Gutiérrez, K., Bien, A., Selland, M. & Pierce, D. (2011). Polylingual and polycultural learning ecologies: mediating emergent academic literacies for dual language learners. *Journal of Early Childhood Literacy*, *11*(2), 232–261.

Hammett, R. (2007). Assessment and new literacies. *E-Learning and Digital Media*, *4*(3), 343–354.

Harris, R. (2000). *Rethinking writing*. London: Continuum.

Hatch, M. (2014). *The maker movement manifesto: rules for innovation in the new world of crafters, hackers and tinkerers*. New York: McGraw Hill Education.

Hattie, J. (2008). *Visible learning*. New York: Routledge.

Heath, S. (1982). What no bedtime story means: narrative skills at home and school. *Language in Society*, *11*(1), 49–76.

Hobbs, R. (2013). Improvisation and strategic risk-taking in informal learning with digital media literacy. *Learning, Media and Technology*, *38*(2), 182–197.

Hollett, T. & Ehret, C. (2015). 'Bean's World': (Mine) Crafting affective atmospheres of gameplay, learning, and care in a children's hospital. *New Media and Society*, *17*(11), 1849–1866.

Hollett, T. & Ehret, C. (2017). *Relational methodologies for mobile literacies: intra-action, rhythm, and atmosphere*. In C. Burnett, G. Merchant, A. Simpson, & M. Walsh (Eds). The Case of the ipad: Mobile Literacies in Education (pp. 227 –244). Singapore: Springer.

Hope, A. (2013). The politics of online risk and the discursive construction of school 'e-Safety'. In N. Selwyn & K. Facer (Eds), *The politics of education and technology: conflicts, controversies, and connections* (pp. 83–98). New York: Palgrave Macmillan.

Horst, H. (2008). Blurring the boundaries: connectivity, convergence and communication in the new media ecology. *Beyond Current Horizons*, 1–12.

Intellectual property Office (2014). *Exceptions to copyright*. Available at: https://www.gov.uk/guidance/exceptions-to-copyright (accessed 18 April 2018).

Ito, M., Gutiérrez, K., Livingstone, S., Penuel, B., Rhodes, J., Salen, K., Schor, Sefton-Green, J., Watkins, S.C. (2013). Connected Learning: An Agenda for Research and Design. Irvine, CA: Digital Media and Learning Research Hub.

Ito, M., Horst, H.A., Bittanti, M., Stephenson, B.H., Lange, P.G., Pascoe, C.J., Robinson, L., Baumer, S., Cody, R., Mahendran, D. & Martínez, K.Z. (2008). *Living and learning with new media: summary of findings from the Digital Youth Project*. Cambridge, MA: MIT Press.

Ito, M. et al. (2009). *Hanging out, messing around, and geeking out: kids living and learning with new media*. Cambridge, MA: MIT Press.

Janks, H. (2010). *Literacy and power*. London: Routledge.

Jenkins, H., Clinton, K., Purushotma, R., Robison, A. J. & Weigel, M. (2006). *Confronting the challenges of participatory culture: media education for the 21st century*. Chicago: MacArthur Foundation.

Jenkins, H., Clinton K., Purushotma, R., Robison, A.J. & Weigel, M. (2009). *Confronting the challenges of participatory culture: media education for the 21st century*. Cambridge, MA: MIT Press.

Kafai, Y. (2010). World of Whyville: an introduction to tween virtual life. *Games and Culture*, 5(1), 3–22.

Keen, A. (2015). *The Internet is not the answer*. London: Atlantic Books.

Kell, C. (2017). *Ways with words and objects: transcontextual and sociomaterial approaches in literacy studies*. 3rd World Congress of Applied Linguistics, Rio de Janeiro, 23–29 July.

Kell, C. & Patrick, D. (2015). Objects, language and trans-contextual communication: introduction to special issue. *Social Semiotics*, 25(4), 387–400.

Kellner, D. & Share, J. (2007). Critical media is not an option. *Learning Inquiry*, 1(1), 59–69.

Kendrick, M. Early, M. & Chemjor, W. (2013). Integrated literacies in a rural Kenyan girls' secondary school journalism club. *Research in the Teaching of English*, 47(4) 391–419.

Kendrick, M., Early, M. & Chemjor, W. (2017). *Play, performance and new literacies in an after-school journalism club in Kenya*. Paper presented at 3rd World Congress of Applied Linguistics, Rio de Janeiro, 23–29 July.

Knobel, M. & Kalman, J. (Eds) (2016). *New literacies and teacher learning: professional development and the digital turn*. New York: Peter Lang.

Kress, G. (2003). *Literacy in the new media age*. London: Routledge.

Kucirkova, N., Messer, D., Sheehy, K. & Flewitt, R. (2013). Sharing personalised stories on iPads: a close look at one parent–child interaction. *Literacy*, 47(3), 115–122.

KZero (2015). Available at: http://www.kzero.co.uk/blog/category/radar-chart (accessed 26 July 2017).

Lammers, J., Magnifico, A. & Curwood, J.S. (2017). Literate identities in fan-based online affinity spaces. In K. Mills, A. Stornaiuolo, A. Smith & J.Z. Pandya (Eds), *Handbook of writing, literacies and education in digital cultures* (pp. 50–62). New York: Routledge.

Lankshear, C. & Knobel, M. (2011). *New literacies: everyday practices and social learning* (3rd Edition). Maidenhead: Open University Press.

Lave, J. & Wenger, E. (1991). *Situated learning: legitimate peripheral participation*. Cambridge: Cambridge University Press.

Leander, K. & Ehret, C. (Eds) (2018). *Affect in literacy learning and teaching: pedagogies, politics, and coming to know*. New York: Routledge.

Leander, K.M. & McKim, K.K. (2003). Tracing the everyday 'sitings' of adolescents on the internet: a strategic adaptation of ethnography across online and offline Spaces. *Education, Communication and Information*, 3(2), 211–240.

Lessig, L. (2002). *Free culture: the nature and future of creativity*. London: Penguin Books.

Lessig, L. (2003). *The future of ideas: the fate of the commons in a connected world*. New York: Random House.

Leu, D., Forzani, E., Burlingame, C., Kulikowich, J., Sedransk, N., Coiro, J. & Kennedy, C. (2013). The new literacies of online research and comprehension: assessing and preparing students for the 21st century with Common Core State Standards. In S. Neuman and L. Gambrell (Eds), *Quality reading instruction in the age of Common Core standards* (pp. 219–236). Newark: International Reading Association.

Leu, D.J., Forzani, E., Rhoads, C., Maykel, C., Kennedy, C. & Timbrell, N. (2015). The new literacies of online research and comprehension: rethinking the reading achievement gap. *Reading Research Quarterly, 50*(1), 37.

Levy, R. (2010). *Young children reading at home and at school*. London: Sage.

Lewis, J. (2005). *Penguin special: the life and times of Allen Lane*. London: Penguin Books.

Littleton, K. & Mercer, N. (2013). *Interthinking: putting talk to work*. Abingdon: Routledge.

Livingstone, S. (2009). *Children and the Internet: great expectations, challenging realities*. Cambridge: Polity.

Livingstone, S. & Haddon, L. (2009) *EU Kids Online: final report, LSE*. London: EU Kids Online.

Livingstone, S. & Helsper, E. (2007). Gradations in digital inclusion: children, young people and the digital divide. *New Media and Society, 9*(4), 671–696.

Lockerington, H., Fisher, S., Jenson, J. & Lindo, L.M. (2016). Professional development from the inside out: redesigning learning through collaborative action research. In M. Knobel & J. Kalman (Eds). *New literacies and teacher learning: professional development and the digital turn* (pp. 65–88). New York: Peter Lang.

Luke, A. (2012). After the testing: talking and reading and writing the world. *Journal of Adolescent and Adult Literacy, 56*(1), 8–13.

Mackey, M. (2002). *Literacies across media: playing the text*. New York: Routledge.

Mackey, M. (2017). Television as a medium. In B. Parry, C. Burnett & G. Merchant (Eds), *Literacy, media, technology: past, present and future* (pp. 25–40). London: Bloomsbury.

Magnifico, A., Curwood, J. & Lammers, J. (2015). Words on the screen: broadening analyses of interactions among fanfiction writers and reviewers. *Literacy, 49*(3), 158–166.

Maine, F. (2017). Collaborative and dialogic meaning-making: how children engage and immerse in the storyworld of a mobile game. In C. Burnett, G. Merchant, A. Simpson & M. Walsh (Eds), *The case of the iPad: mobile literacies in education* (pp. 211–225). Singapore: Springer.

Marsh, J. (2010). Young children's play in online virtual worlds. *Journal of Early Childhood Research, 8*(1), 23–39.

Marsh, J. (2016). Unboxing videos: co-construction of the child as cyberflâneur. *Discourse: Studies in the Cultural Politics of Education, 37*(3), 369–380.

Marsh, J., Plowman, L., Yamada-Rice, D., Bishop, J., Lahmar, J., Scott, F., Davenport, A., Davis, S., French, K., Piras, M., Thornhill, S., Robinson, P. & Winter, P. (2015). *Exploring play and creativity in pre-schoolers' use of apps: final project report*. Available at: http://www.techandplay.org (accessed 10 January 2016).

Massumi, B. (2002). *Parables for the virtual: movement, affect, sensation.* London: Duke University Press.

Merchant, G. (2007a). Writing the future in the digital age. *Literacy, 41*(3), 118–128.

Merchant, G. (2007b). Mind the gap(s): discourses and discontinuity in digital literacies. *E-Learning and Digital Media, 4*(3), 241–255.

Merchant, G. (2009). Literacy in virtual worlds. *Journal of Research in Reading, 32*(1), 38–56.

Merchant, G. (2013a). The trashmaster: literacy and new media. *Language and Education, 27*(2), 144–160.

Merchant, G. (2013b). 'I oversee what the children are doing': challenging literacy pedagogy in virtual worlds. In G. Merchant, J. Gillen, J. Marsh & J. Davies (Eds), *Virtual literacies: interactive spaces for children and young people* (pp. 161–178). New York: Routledge.

Merchant, G. (2015a). Moving with the times: how mobile digital literacies are changing childhood. In V. Duckworth & G. Ade-Ojo (Eds), *Landscapes of specific literacies in contemporary society: exploring a social model of literacy* (pp. 103–116). London: Routledge.

Merchant, G. (2015b). Apps, adults and young children: researching digital literacy practices in context. In R. Jones, A. Chik & C. Hafner (Eds), *Discourse and digital practices: doing discourse analysis in the digital age* (pp. 144–158). New York: Routledge.

Merchant, G. (2016). Virtual worlds and online videogames for children and young people: promises and challenges. In M. Lesley & B. Guzzetti (Eds), *The handbook of research on the societal impact of social media* (pp. 291–316). New York: IGI Global.

Merchant, G. (2017). Hands, fingers and iPads. In C. Burnett, G. Merchant, A. Simpson & M. Walsh (Eds). *The case of the iPad: mobile literacies in education* (pp. 245–257). Singapore: Springer.

Ministère de l'Éducation et de l'Enseignement supérieur (2017). *Progression of learning in elementary school.* Available at: http://www1.education.gouv.qc.ca/progressionprimaire/index_en.asp (accessed 10 July 2017).

Monkhouse, J., Bailey, C., Baker, W., Power, D., Bailey, C., Burnett, C., Daniels, K. & Merchant, G. (2017). Word on the street. *English 4-11*, Spring, *59*, 17–20.

Moss, G. (2012). Literacy policy and English/literacy practice: researching the interaction between different knowledge fields. *English Teaching: Practice and Critique, 11*(1), 104–120.

Moss, G. (2017). Assessment, accountability and the literacy curriculum: reimagining the future in the light of the past. *Literacy, 54*(2), 56–64.

Moyles J. (1989). *Just playing.* Buckingham: Open University Press.

Nikolopoulou, K. & Gialamas, V. (2015). Barriers to the integration of computers in early childhood settings: teachers' perceptions. *Education and Information Technologies, 20*(2), 285–301.

O'Mara, J. (2017). Narratives come to life through coding: digital game making as language and literacy curriculum. In C. Beavis, M. Dezuanni & J. O'Mara (Eds), *Serious play: literacy, learning and digital games* (pp. 102–113). London: Routledge.

O'Neill, C. (1995). *Drama worlds: a framework*. Portsmouth, NH: Heinemann.

OECD (2011). *PISA 2009 Results: Students on line: Digital technologies and performance Vol VI*. Available at: http://www.oecd.org/edu/school/programme forinternationalstudentassessmentpisa/pisa2009resultsstudentsonlinedigital technologiesandperformancevolumevi.htm (accessed 18 April 2018).

OECD (2017). *OECD PISA financial literacy assessment of students*. Available at: http://www.oecd.org/daf/fin/financial-education/launch-pisa-financial-literacy-students-2017.htm (accessed 10 July 2017).

Ofcom (2016). *Children's media lives*. Available at: https://www.ofcom.org.uk/ research-and-data/media-literacy-research/childrens/childrens-media-lives (accessed 10 January 2017).

Ofcom (2017). *Internet use and attitudes*. Available at: https://www.ofcom.org.uk/ research-and-data/internet-and-on-demand-research/internet-use-and-attitudes (accessed 10 December 2017).

Opie, I. & Opie, P. (1969). *Children's games in street and playground*. Oxford: Clarendon Press.

Otsuji, E. & Pennycook, A. (2010). Metrolingualism: fixity, fluidity and language in flux. *International Journal of Multilingualism, 7*(3), 240–254.

Palmer, S. (2006). *Toxic childhood: how the modern world is damaging our children and what we can do about it*. London: Orion.

Parry, B. (2013). *Children, film and literacy*. London: Palgrave Macmillan.

Pearce, C. & Artemesia (2010). *Communities of play: emergent cultures in multiplayer games and virtual worlds*. Cambridge: MIT Press.

Penuel, W. & DiGiacomo, D. (2017). Connected learning. In K. Peppler (Ed.), *The Sage encyclopedia of out-of-school learning* (pp. 132–134). London: Sage.

Peppler, K. (2013). Social media and creativity. In D. Lemish (Ed.), *Routledge international handbook of children, adolescents, and media* (pp. 193–200). New York: Routledge.

Peppler, K., Halverson, E. & Kafai, Y. (2016). *Makeology: makerspaces as learning environments*. New York: Routledge.

Pew Internet Studies (2017) *Internet and technology*. Available at: http://www. pewinternet.org (accessed 20 May 2017).

Playful Learning Center (2015). *Manifesto: playing with learning*. Available at: https://helda.helsinki.fi/bitstream/handle/10138/158664/Manifesto_2015_ PLC.pdf?sequence=1.

Plum (2017). Accidentally on purpose. *The Harry Potter Fan Fiction Site*. Available at: https://harrypotterfanfiction.com.

Potter, J. & Gilje, O. (2015). Curating as a new literacy practice. *E-Learning and Digital Media, 12*(2), 123–127.

Prinsloo, M. (2005). The new literacies as placed resources. *Perspectives in Education, 23*(4), 87–98.

QCA (2004). *More than words: multimodal texts in the classroom*. London: QCA.

QCA (2005). *More than words 2: Creating stories on page and screen*. London: QCA.

Rautio, P. & Jokinen, P. (2016). Children's relations to the more-than-human world beyond developmental views. In Evans R. Horton J., Skelton T. (Eds), *Play and Recreation, Health and Wellbeing* (35–49). Singapore: Springer.

Razfar, A. & Gutiérrez, K. (2013). Reconceptualizing early childhood literacy: the sociocultural influence and new directions in digital and hybrid mediation. In J. Larson & J. Marsh (Eds), *The Sage Handbook of early childhood literacy* (pp. 52–79). London: Sage.

Reckwitz, A. (2002). Towards a theory of social practices: a development in culturalist theorizing. *European Journal of Social Theory, 5*(2), 243–263.

Robles-de-la-Torre, G. (2006). The importance of the sense of touch in virtual and real environments. *IEEE Multimedia, 13*(3), 24–30.

Rowe, D. & Miller, M. (2017). The affordances of touchscreen tablets and digital cameras for young children's multimodal, multilingual composing. In C. Burnett, G. Merchant, A. Simpson & M. Walsh (Eds), *Mobile literacies in education: the case of the iPad* (pp. 159–178). Singapore: Springer.

Rvachew, S. (2017). *Re-visiting the digital divide: collective responsibilities and individual responses.* Keynote, DigilitEY EU Cost Action meeting, 1st September.

Salomaa, S. & Mertala, P. (forthcoming) *Early learining in the Digital Age: Digital Pedagogy and Early childhood.* In I. Palaiologu & C. Eray (Eds) *Digital practices in early childhood.* London: Sage.

Schatzki, T. (2002). *The site of the social.* University Park, Pennyslvania: Pennsylvania University Press.

Serafini, F. (2012). Expanding the four resources model: reading visual and multimodal texts. *Pedagogies: An International Journal, 7*(2), 150–164.

Silvers, P., Shorey, M. & Crafton, L. (2010). Critical literacies in a primary multiliteracies classroom: the Hurricane Group. *Journal of Early Childhood Literacy, 10*(4), 379–409.

Simpson, A. & Walsh, M. (2017). Multimodal layering: students learning with iPads in primary school classrooms. In C. Burnett, G. Merchant, A. Simpson & M. Walsh (Eds), *The case of the iPad: mobile literacies in education* (pp. 67–85). Singapore: Springer.

Squire, K. & Steinkuehler, C. (2017). The problem with screen time. *Teachers College Review,* 119(11).

St Pierre, E.A. (2014). An always already absent collaboration. *Cultural Studies ↔ Critical Methodologies, 14*(4), 374–379.

Steinkuehler, C. (2007). Massively multiplayer online games as a constellation of literacy practices. *E-Learning and Digital Media, 4*(3), 297–318.

Stornaiuolo, A. (2016). Teaching in global collaborations: navigating challenging conversations through cosmopolitan activity. *Teaching and Teacher Education, 59,* 503–513.

Stornaiuolo, A., Hull, G. & Hall, M. (2017). Cosmopolitan practices, networks and flows of literacies. In K. Mills, A. Stornaiuolo, A. Smith & J.Z. Pandya (Eds), *Handbook of writing, literacies, and education in digital cultures* (pp. 13–25). New York: Routledge.

Street, B.V. (1984). *Literacy in theory and practice.* Cambridge: Cambridge University Press.

Sutton-Smith, B. (1987) *The ambiguity of play.* Cambridge, MA: Harvard University Press.

Swain, F. (2011). Susan Greenfield: living online is changing our brains. Interview in *New Scientist,* 27 July. Available at: https://www.newscientist.com/article/

mg21128236-400-susan-greenfield-living-online-is-changing-our-brains (accessed 18 April 2018).

Takacs, Z.K., Swart, E.K. & Bus, A.G. (2015). Benefits and pitfalls of multimedia and interactive features in technology-enhanced storybooks. *Review of Educational Research*, 85(4), 698–739.

Taylor, R. (2006) Actions speak as loud as words: a multimodal analysis of boys' talk in the classroom. *English in Education*, 40(3), 66–82.

Taylor, R. (2012). Messing about with metaphor: multimodal aspects to children's creative meaning making. *Literacy*, 46(3), 156–166.

Taylor, R. (2014). Meaning between, in and around words, gestures and postures – multimodal meaning-making in children's classroom discourse. *Language and Education*, 28(5), 401–420.

Tolmie, A.K., Topping, K.J., Christie, D., Donaldson, C., Howe, C., Jessiman, E., Livingston, K. & Thurston, A. (2010). Social effects of collaborative learning in primary schools. *Learning and Instruction*, 20(3), 177–191.

UK Safer Internet Centre (2018). Available at: https://www.saferinternet.org.uk (accessed 18 April 2018).

Vasquez, C. (2014). *The discourse of online consumer reviews*. London: Bloomsbury.

Vincent, D. (2000). *The rise of mass literacy: reading and writing in modern Europe*. Cambridge: Polity.

vTech UK (2017). *vTech Baby*. Available at: http://www.vtechuk.com/vtech-baby (accessed 18 April 2018).

Waller, M. (2013). More than tweets: developing the 'new' and 'old' through online social networks. In G. Merchant, J. Gillen, J. Marsh & J. Davies (Eds), *Virtual literacies* (pp. 126–141). London: Routledge.

Waring, H.Z. (2013). Doing being playful in the second language classroom. *Applied Linguistics*, 34(2), 191–210.

Wells, G. (1987). *The meaning makers: children learning language and learning to use language*. London: Hodder & Stoughton.

Wiliam, D. (2011). *Embedded formative assessment*. Bloomington, IN: Solution Tree Press.

Willett, R., Richards, C., Marsh, J., Burn, A. & Bishop, J. (2013). *Children, media and playground cultures: ethnographic studies of school playtimes*. Basingstoke: Palgrave.

Wohlwend, K. (2013). *Literacy playshop: new literacies, popular media, and play in the early childhood classroom*. New York: Teachers College Press.

Wohlwend, K. & Buchholz, B. (2014). Paper pterodactyls and popsicle sticks: expanding school literacy through filmmaking and toymaking. In C. Burnett, J. Davies, G. Merchant & J. Rowsell (Eds), *New literacies around the globe: policy and pedagogy* (pp. 33–49). London: Routledge.

Woo, M.M., Chu, S.K.W. & Li, X. (2013). Peer-feedback and revision process in a wiki mediated collaborative writing. *Educational Technology Research and Development*, 61(2), 279–309.

Wrigley, T. (2016). Not so simple: the problem with 'evidence-based practice' and the EEF toolkit. *Forum*, 58(2), 237–252.

Yamada-Rice, D. (2014). The semiotic landscape and 3-year-olds' emerging under-standing of multimodal communication practices. *Journal of Early Childhood Research*, 12(2), 154–184.

INDEX